Ernest L. Norman
Author, philosopher, poet, scientist, director,
moderator of Unarius Science of Life

UNARIUS
UNiversal ARticulate Interdimensional

Understanding of Science

COSMIC

CONTINUUM

COSMIC CONTINUUM

By
Ernest L. Norman

Third Edition

Published By
UNARIUS, SCIENCE OF LIFE
P.O. Box 1042
El Cajon, Calif. 92020

Other Works by Ernest L. Norman

The Infinite Concept of Cosmic Creation
    Thirteen lesson study course
    Advanced lesson course
    The key to the Unarius science

The Pulse of Creation Series:

The Voice of Venus	Vol.1
The Voice of Eros	Vol.2
The Voice of Hermes	Vol.3
The Voice of Orion	Vol.4
The Voice of Muse	Vol.5

Infinite Contact
Infinite Perspectus
Tempus Procedium
Tempus Invictus
Tempus Interludium Vol.-I
Tempus Interludium Vol.-II
The Truth About Mars
The Elysium (Parables)
The Anthenium (Poetry)

The True Life of Jesus
The Story of the Little Red Box
    (By Unarius' Students & E. L. Norman)

Bridge to Heaven
    The Revelations of Ruth Norman, by Ruth Norman

PREFACE

In the histories of the world, it is invariably acknowledged that all good, all great achievements and advanced forms of culture were given in posterity to mankind by certain individuals who were equally advanced in their particular idiom. Many of these great souls have died for this cause of moral, mental and physical freedom; others have remained anonymous through the passage of time until the day of vindication when mankind acknowledged their creativeness by common usage.

In line with this preface, we present this book, "Cosmic Continuum", a most amazing and remarkable book, also dedicated to the future generations of mankind who will, in their posterity, find common usage for all principles and concepts contained in its pages.

Indeed, it will be so mandated that if mankind is to survive in a progressive continuity upon the face of this planet, he will, by the necessity for survival, be forced to use and adapt in common usage, these principles and concepts just as have other races of peoples on other planets in far-off solar systems.

Equally remarkable or even more amazing, is the manner in which this book was brought into existence and one which bespeaks the highly developed and trained aptitude of the human mind which can use as its source, the vast wealth of information contained in the Higher Mental Superconscious. The manner of creating this book was achieved by the author in his usual method, by dictation, using a tape recorder. This entire book was dictated in one continuous session, save for a few brief pauses and total elapsed recording time was nine hours, completely filling both tracks of two standard 7 inch reels of tape and was transcribed and printed verbatim, requiring no sentence structure changes. There was no preparation for this dictation, in fact, not even a premonition; the author simply sat down and began to dictate.

When you have finished reading this book, you will agree that it is indeed a prodigious mental feat and one which is without equal. For in this consideration, we must remember that the concepts given are far in advance of our present-day scientific technocracy; scientific concepts which have just begun to be vaguely explored by a few of the more far-reaching minds.

"Cosmic Continuum" will therefore, in the future, become one of the classics of scientific literature and along with other works posed by the same author, will also become the reference library used by the scientist of the future millennium.

It might be well to note that this book carries the same transcending power often felt by those who read the works of Unarius; a power often causing drowsiness, lassitude or felt as heat; and should this occur to you, it is not the context of reading material but, through these words, you have become attuned to this great source of healing and adjusting power.

Remember also that inasmuch as these principles and concepts are extremely advanced, they will bear *much repeat reading* and the subsequent benefits gained from such rereading will be felt in many different ways. Your mental horizon will be broadened, you will find better adjustment in your material world; physical healing will be manifested and peace of mind will take the place of the chaotic misunderstandings of yesterday.

COSMIC CONTINUUM

PART ONE

CHAPTER 1

In common abstractions based on our nuclear science, all matter can be resolved into energy. Therefore, in the pure idiom, this energy is part of the sum and total of what is commonly referred to as spirit. In other words, interdimensional forms of energy, manner of transmissional factors of dynamics, and the appearance of energy as seemingly solid matter— are all part of these abstractions. Consequently, it can be universally resolved that as all is energy, and as energy is dynamic, all action must therefore first take place in these seemingly invisible dimensions. This is just as true with man and his course of life as it is with the atomic constituents which make up his body.

Consciousness in daily life is therefore an integrated pattern of relationships with numerous past transmissions of life as well as past lifetimes. These

1

relationships, moving as oscillating patterns harmonically attuned to consciousness, can be pictured as various formations of sine wave energies. These past life experience relationships represent, in scientific parlance, the negative polarity of life.

As all polarities must be equated into two basic and diametrically opposed opposites, we must therefore have with this negative side of life, a positive pole which gives not only a basic equilibrium, but it is that which makes all common forms of energy transmission possible. A universally recognized concept of this positive polarity relates the individual to the various inspirational aggregates which he finds in his daily life. Such aggregates are the various religious systems, pantheologies, etc., which he has always automatically regarded as spiritual in nature.

Obviously, as is posed by the negative polarity referred to as the subconsciousness and which composes by far the largest part of the ego, the individual must then have a positive polarity which can be represented as the Spiritual Ego. Jesus referred to the Spiritual Ego as the "Father Within". This Ego, through frequency relationship, resolves itself into an infinite number of forms of consciousness which will, through the common interchange of polarity patterns, thus be joined in a common union of associations.

This common joining does two things: it neutralizes caustic negative effects which always subsequently occur in future happenings to this individual and it also polarizes the corresponding idiom of consciousness in the Superego. The individual will then, in the concourse of thousands of lives, develop this Spiritual Ego into such proportions that it becomes the dominant polarity in his life. Such a person can thus be said to be overshadowed by a Superhuman Being; thus he will then reflect into his daily earth life such attributes as were expressed in the life of Jesus. For, in that individual, we can find a true example of this highly developed Spiritual Overself reflecting through and influencing the physical life in various acts which the physical man has termed Godlike.

The average person then, who is seeking truth and an escape from the material world with its purgatory of karma, must always carry foremost in his mind the vision of the Higher Self; he must give it every opportunity to guide him in his daily life. He must also use it only with the most positive solutions and wiser attitudes toward various life experiences for only in positive consciousness is the Superego developed. Thus the Superego becomes the master over the lower negative self; and it can then be said that this person has been "saved" by Christ—his own Christ Self.

Because of certain statements and concepts postulated in the previous text, the average reader may wish to challenge these statements. He may feel reluctant to give up the age-old concept of the "divine intercession", as it has been constantly indoctrinated in his various beliefs and pantheologies and which he has acquired over his period of evolution.

The idea of "divine intercession" represents to most people a very convenient relief and, as such, an escape mechanism from the various otherwise insoluble differences, in man's daily life. He has been subconsciously, or consciously, believing that no matter how tough the going was, should things pile up against him, the "divine intercession", the belief that Christ could save him, would immediately dissolve everything in that forthcoming "judgment day".

Moreover, the context of the previous portion of this chapter is also quite complex in nature, for it immediately presents the problem to the reader that he now has to assume the position of the guiding power in his own destiny. He must also assume the moral responsibility for all acts of consciousness and this, too, could cause a revolt in the reader's mind. He may then refer to one or more incidents in his own daily life where he believes spiritual healing has been instigated; or he may even refer to the classical example of the great Avatar, Jesus of Nazareth, who healed so many people.

For these reasons, therefore, we shall take this classical lifetime of Jesus as a typical example, as it is portrayed in the so-called art of "divine healing", as the life of this man is quite well-known to some 800 million people who call themselves Christians. Contrary to general opinion, Jesus did not heal or help to heal everyone or all with whom He came in contact, who were in need of healing or of some corrective measure. For every one who received results, there were hundreds who went away in dire straits and circumstances and were not helped in any way, at least not at that time, by any action which they wished might have taken place.

The reasons for this situation are quite obvious when properly understood. As has been previously postulated, healing can take place in the physical or material worlds only as a result of certain cyclic junctions and which, when this takes place, automatically create within the person, the desired healing results.

Such conditions always are, and always have been, an automatic function within the mind and body of every individual. The very fact that life is sustained from the automation of this same principle is quite easily explained and fully justified in everyday life.

However, to understand fully, it is most necessary that the student learn of certain fundamental principles which can be referred to as creative and re-creative transmissions which are in constant force and activation in the Infinite Cosmos around him. This is all part of the Infinite Mind to which most people

4

refer as God.

To the scientist and those who understand the scientific principles underlying the various transmissions of life and also in such fields which are referred to as atomic structures, these concepts and principles will be more easily understood. However, it is most necessary in all cases, before healing or readjustment in life can take place, that certain fundamental values in these creative principles be at least somewhat understood.

Referring again to the previous context, it was resolved in common physical science that all substance, visible or invisible, is energy. This also includes those seemingly so-called particles of matter, termed atoms, which are actually energy solar systems. In the various interdimensional linkages, it is not possible for any third dimensional transmission of life—as it is seen about us—to take place without immediate and connecting reactions with an infinite number of dimensions from which the very source of life and power stems. It is impossible to do one of the simpler acts of daily life without having implications which reach hundreds of thousands of years, in the term or sense of time, both into the past and into the future, so far as the relationship of energy and its transmission is concerned.

Therefore, we must consider the mechanics of these various transmissions which we call the appearances of life about us. First, it can always be pictured and assumed, in the dynamics of these transmissions, that all things travel as a sine wave or a combination of such wave frequencies and sine waves always vibrate; or from the polarities as are so contained from positive to negative in these sine wave formations, they are carrying a certain consciousness within them. These various appearances from positive to negative and the relationship of this consciousness takes place at a predetermined rate of time or frequency.

To Einstein and such savants, the transference of energy from the third dimensional planes—or the material world—into other nearby planes such as the fourth or fifth dimension, where it seems time actually merges and becomes a quality or a quantity of the transmission of energy, has always posed a great mystery. To the student, this principle is much more easily understood than are these various contexts or the theses to such theorems as are contained in the postulations by Einstein.

We simply envision the fourth dimension as such a world or a dimension in which the transmission of life always takes place as cyclic motion within whatever energy wave forms we are so concerned; or in other words, simply as a circle. Many years ago, Einstein was quoted as saying that if you drew a line far enough and straight enough, it would meet itself coming around at the other end. This is, in a sense, his fourth dimensional concept and, to some degree, fully proves what we are about to discuss.

In other words, so far as other worlds and dimensions are concerned, any particular idea, form, or consciousness, as it is related to the Infinite Mind, is complete in itself, and therefore can be considered cyclic in motion. It is the vast conjunctive relationships of an infinite number of these different types and forms of consciousness which go to make up the matrix of the Infinite Cosmos that we call the cosmogony about us. It is also the various differences and alliances with these cyclic patterns as they are concerned with the sinasoidal wave forms of which they are composed which go to make up the great vortical patterns, patterns which make up suns and solar systems. They also make up the very atoms of our physical bodies.

We have fully established the relationship in which all things can be resolved into energy, and conduct themselves according to certain principles which, for the sake of introspection, can be called laws. The word "law" is referred to loosely as merely a convenient or a descriptive word, for in all cases "principle", as it is concerned with the Infinite Mind, is a much better form of terminology.

The various wave form transmissions, as they are concerned in the oscillating processes both finitely and infinitely, always function (as it has been stated), according to these well-known laws. In other words, our first law is concerned with what is commonly referred to as harmonic relationship. When we find that two different wave forms strike each other or that they intermingle—there is a third set of wave forms generated which are called harmonic structures or harmonic wave forms. This third set of wave form patterns always carry, to some degree, the original idiom or consciousness of the primary elements which instigated the harmonic formation. Therefore, as such regenerative processes are subjective to the numerous different conditions and alliances with similar wave forms in compatible rates of frequency with which they might become interrelated; this presents a rather complex problem which could become quite confusing.

It must be remembered that, conversely, the same law applies to keep all things in their proper dimension and their proper relationship without this so-called confusion; for diametrically opposed to the law of harmonic principle and as a balancing agent is the law of frequency relationship which determines that, according to the rate of vibration, any energy wave is either in compatible relationship with another wave or it is diametrically opposed or opposite to it, and under no condition can it merge with this other wave form until it has adjusted its rate of frequency. This principle then, after it has been thoroughly established in the reader's mind, leads us to another principle which is directly concerned with such frequency affiliations, and is of particular value when we wish to understand more thoroughly the action of the solid or atomic world about us.

This is the principle which modern science calls catalysis, or the catalytic action of a third or neutral element in conjunction with two or more other elements which, up to that time, have not been synonymous or compatible in nature. Catalytic action means that we must now transfer the perspective of our analysis to the very atom itself and realize that all atoms, large and small—either as they have been compounded in molecules or exist in a singular fashion—always have one common property: that is, they have a field of force. As they are electrically constituted from various positive and negative charges revolving around a common nucleus or core, they are also radiating into the space about them, various wave forms of energy which are the direct result of these different regenerations within the atom itself.

Some atoms, such as radium, actually shoot or fire off tiny bullets of pure energy from the very heart of the atom itself, in a common process of degeneration. The field of force around each atom, whether it is large or small, is governed directly by the same laws of harmonic relationship or frequency vibration as are those dynamically inclined, such as the free-moving interchange or interplay of energy formations within the range of the more commonly accepted forms of energy which we may see about us.

If we take common ordinary table salt, we shall find a classical example of what is termed catalytic action, for table salt involves the combination of two elements which, under normal conditions, are entirely foreign to each other's nature and could not in any other way be so combined. These two common elements are the deadly gas chlorine and the common inert substance known as sodium. By catalytic action in nature's great laboratories, due to several compelling agents of force such as are contained in sunlight and other catalytic agents, the gas and sodium come in contact with one another and at proper conjunctions the two atoms are merged in a common union with a simple free electron in their orbit of transmission, thus becoming the inert substance known as salt.

Thereby, these two atoms are constantly so interlocked with this electronic constituent that they have completely neutralized their original and determining qualities as atoms in their own particular scale of atomic weights. Either chlorine or sodium would be a poison in the human system and could cause distress or death; but merged as salt, become instead, one of the agents used by the body to maintain a certain alkaline balance which is so necessary in the process of osmosis in the lymphatic system.

This same action takes place when an individual swallows an aspirin tablet. The tiny atoms as they are combined in molecules, when reaching certain different portions of the lower brain structures—which are in control of such centers called the pain centers— immediately neutralize with their field of force the impulses of energy which are called pain. Thus they have that analgesic action which is sought by those who are suffering from some simple form of pain, such as a headache.

The catalytic action or the combining or the recombining of various fields of force, as they are so visualized in various atomic or molecular structures, can also be carried on up into the infinite cosmogony. There it will be found that the same relationship exists, not only in planetary systems, but also in such structures which the astronomer calls universes or galaxies. The same particular affiliations and transmissions of energy structures as are contained in the atom exist, in a pure sense, in a much more expanded and larger ratio of transmission.

CHAPTER 2

Now we have begun to understand that even in the simplest and most common acts of everyday life, there are always some very scientific principles involved which make these acts possible and that these various transmissions have, as has been suggested, very far-reaching and infinite effects. They relate not only to the immediate appearance as they are concerned with the individual but in a sense they also can affect, either inversely or adversely, certain dimensional transmissions which may be hundreds of thousands of years in the past or in the future. It is in these common transmissions of everyday life, in the affiliation of frequency relationships and such common abstractions as resolve themselves into the individual's constructive evolutionary process which he calls life, which have been the determining elements in what he calls sin or evil, and good.

We can consider that any act which is performed by the individual is, first and primarily, merely the transmission or the release of a certain amount of energy. The energy used by the farmer to hold his plowshare in the furrow can be the same energy which the same man could use with a sword to strike off an adversary's head. It is in the transmission of these various energy formations with which the average individual is concerned in his evolutionary process from life to life; it is he, himself, who determines which is or which is not constructive in his evolutionary pattern.

Thus it is, sooner or later, every individual reaches that certain particular threshold within his own consciousness when he becomes tremendously conscious of the difference between good and evil. When he is thus concerned personally with various transmissions of an evil nature in his past lives, he may say to himself that he has been destructively inclined. This, then, will always cause the individual a great sense of guilt, even though in his material life he cannot explain its origin to anyone; for it is a complex structure of various energy wave forms which are oscillating in his psychic body which have, at that particular moment, created for him a great subconscious sense of guilt. Whether or not he was directly responsible for these different energy wave forms— as they are impinged in the psychic body in his transmission of life in the past—is no justifiable excuse but merely means he lived his life in the common idiom of that particular moment; and in that process the energy wave forms entered into the structural matrix of the psychic self. He will, therefore, under these common conditions have a great urgency, a feeling from within himself that he must by some means cancel out or relieve the psychic pressure of this great guilt mechanism.

As is posed in the previous context, this feeling comes from and is primarily instigated by the development of his other polarity, the superconsciousness, for in these opposites of relationships, the individual is immediately struck with these great differences. The fact is, primarily, that the individual lives most of the time in the spiritual worlds anyway, where he can thus see these diametrically opposed differences.

It can also be resolved that the transmissions of life are always instigated from the spiritual side of man's nature and not in some supposedly immediate superficial reactionary combination of conditions which might arise on the surface of his daily life. Any act of any individual in his continuance of daily life, is also the continued and sustained oscillation which was previously incurred by the individual in other places; and under the laws of harmonic relationships, he is constantly instigating and inflicting within his psychic structures new and other differences in these psychic structures of energy wave forms which can be considered harmonic in nature to the originating wave forms.

Therefore in that particular position of life between earth lives, the person is more conscious of the higher, or the Superconscious Presence in the various affiliations with the more constructive or progressive side of evolution. He wishes then to cancel out these things so that in the particular spiritual worlds, in moments of transcendency, he makes certain connections or affiliations; or he may actually undergo specific scholastic teachings which will show him how these various wave forms can be cancelled out in order that he may be reinstated in a healthier position in his daily life.

We can take any particular person who has reached this threshold and find him traveling in the spiritual worlds and he will, under these conditions, affiliate himself with such teaching schools or agencies. Should he find some Avatar, such as Jesus, teaching a large group of people and showing them how the numerous and varied energy wave forms can be changed or transmuted in their psychic bodies, he will naturally have a great and compelling desire to do so.

However, as part of this teaching curriculum, it is most necessarily imposed in the student's mind that the corrective processes must take place in the same dimensions of relationship in which they were formerly incurred. This is so simply because of frequency relationships, for the person in question must now regenerate a completely new set of wave forms and cyclic patterns. This new set of regenerative wave forms, while compatible as harmonic structures with the original set which was negative in nature, is now of a positive nature. Thus in combining with the original negative wave forms which incurred the indisposition or sin, they will, in this combining process, neutralize—just as in the case of common table salt —the negative or repercussive elements in these various wave forms. This, then, is the principle behind all spiritual healing. As has been previously postulated, it must and always does come from the inner or spiritual side of man's nature.

Referring again to Jesus, the Avatar, and to those whom he contacted and who were so-called "miraculously healed" from various indispositions, this was the recombining of these different scientific principles, as previously explained. Those who were healed recognized in Jesus, the principle or Guiding Force or Avatar, who had formerly contacted them in the Spiritual World and had taught them the principles of correction of the various negative energy wave forms which were in existence in their psychic bodies; whether they were lepers or were blind or were otherwise deformed mentally or physically, made no difference.

In the true light of introspection as they were posed in that spiritual world, and looking into their psychic bodies from the higher self, these people saw the malformed wave form structures residing in their psychic bodies; but, at that time, they had no way or means to dissolve or cancel them, other than to reestablish themselves in an oscillating fashion on the common plane of earth life where they formerly incurred the negative indispositions. When Jesus came by the road where they were thus waiting for him,

14

through frequency vibration, a certain rapport was again established with the life between earth lives where they had seen these energy wave forms and had had explained to them the principles for cancellation.

Referring to these various mental projections—which come under the heading of psychokinesis and which were an aiding or a catalytic agent or force in the process, then recombining as harmonic constituents the energy wave forms so evolved in this process —from the Higher Self of Jesus, these negative wave forms in the psychic body, as they related to atomic structures, were thus cancelled out and completely reconstituted as positive reciprocating elements which could be considered normal in their relationship to the human body. The very atoms, as structural elements in molecular formations and cell formations in the human body, were thus connected or changed instantaneously.

The thought must be held in the mind of the reader that every atom is a sustained or surface appearance of a cyclic pattern as it resolves in that dimension of the psychic body; and this same cyclic relationship also relates to every other atom in the infinite universe. These same principles also hold true in any and all sundry superficial cases of healing such as are incurred in our modern everyday world, whether they take place in the hospitals, in the homes, or under any other condition which can be envisioned by the reader. The same principles which have been explained must always be in proper conjunction and relationship before healing of any sort can take place.

It makes little difference whether the person who is ill or so concerned with healing, visualizes this catalytic agent as Jesus the Avatar, or whether he finds this catalytic and compelling agent in the face of his doctor, or that he finds it in the face of his priest; or perhaps he could even find it by swallowing a simple aspirin tablet or even by drinking a glass of water.

This leads us to the most necessary of all energy wave forms which are, as we have explained, catalytic in nature and which have been rather loosely grouped by the materialist as faith. In the field of relative energy relationships, there is a certain principle (or law), which is constantly and normally functioning in every process of life, called psychokinesis. In a sense, it is quite similar to other principles which have been explained; but it means that any individual can, in the normal processes of thinking, actually attune such frequencies of the regenerative forces of the mind into frequencies which are compatible with some exterior or interior object or transmission of life.

We can find many different classical examples of psychokinesis, whether they are involved in our own personal relationships with life, or whether they are concerned with acts which involve other people. There is no such thing as blind faith, for faith is always a subconscious or an inward knowing—a complete conviction that a certain something can and does exist.

We could not possibly, at any moment, envision anything transpiring unless we knew it was completely possible and actually knew, to some extent—at least inwardly—the mechanics involved in such a happening. This, then, is faith; and whether the individual finds that his healing takes place in the simple act of believing in a fetish or a charm, a pill, or in some individual, makes little or no difference. It merely means that the individual has, through some seemingly subconscious process, connected up the transmissions of various energy wave forms into a continuity which is catalytic in action and thus can change the negative wave forms in the psychic structures. Conversely, the atomic structures will sooner or later follow through and the defect is thus cleared up in the physical body.

And so, dear reader, it makes little or no difference what it is we do, or into what dimensions we can carry our introspection; we shall always find that the same principles, as have been explained—which relate to the transmission of energy wave forms in harmonic structures, catalytic actions and psychokinetic projections—all mean one and the same thing.

These principles are inviolate; they apply not only in our own physical dimension as they are related to our physical life but are the basic and motivating forces which engender all of the processes of life, whether spiritual or material in nature. We shall never at any time find the ending or the cessation of these principles, for they are the energizing, the reactivating, rebuilding agencies and forces which are involved in that ever-expanding, contracting, constructive process we have related to the Infinite Mind which we call God.

Time, therefore, is of little importance; we shall find that only in the material dimension does time become a separate property in the transmission of life about us. Basically our main concern is in the primary purpose of evolution itself, in the creation of the Spiritual Ego to such proportions that it becomes a reciprocating element in the Infinite Mind and the Creative Force, not as a selfish and self-centered agency designed primarily from its own selfish instincts as they were garnered from energy wave forms in more primitive lifetimes, but into constructive evolutionary patterns of thought which are concerned in constructive processes in helping to completely regenerate the Infinite Cosmos in its normal functional activities.

It is conceivable, in the normal process of life, that each individual is concerned with the age-old and primitive process of equilibrium between the so-called negative or evil forces and the positive polarities which are called good or the mystical forces. Inasmuch as this is an age-old problem involving the very beginnings of any one particular individual's life upon the planet earth—or upon any other similar planet— the previous explanations may not have been quite adequate to completely fulfill or justify a corrective process and to instill a new philosophy of life in the individual's mind.

As the struggle between good and evil is age-old, a person may be inclined to ask this direct question: What then becomes of those people who are incorrigibles or who are dominating figures in an evil or negative way? To look back into history, we can find classical examples of these various evil people as they have written certain bloody pages in the history of mankind; such men as the Genghis Khan, Hitler and other figures whose cloaks are dyed with the crimson blood of their fellow men. This does indeed pose a great problem in mental balances as they are concerned with the average individual and he may be confused in the processes of mind in establishing such an equilibrium in his thinking.

He can eventually strike out the words good or evil and instead instill within this consciousness a much more realistic concept which concerns the positive and negative energy wave forms. Referring to this particular establishment of equilibrium, we must therefore revert into the physical world again for a starting place in this introspection. We can, for convenience sake, look directly into the human body itself; there we find that as far as the physical body is concerned, almost all of the processes which sustain life within that body—as they are concerned in a physical sense

—are completely automatic in nature. This automation involves the respiratory system and various digestive processes which in a sense and to a large degree, perform entirely without consciousness on the part of the individual.

Oxygen enters the lungs and causes a certain aeration of the blood stream which is the fundamental functioning principal of the human body; and as far as that goes, of every particular living organism which can be said to have a similarly constructed body. The scientist might say food is burned in the body but this so-called burning process is a misconception, just as are many of the different principles in scientific nomenclature. This means that we have a certain direct transmission of energy from one form to another.

If we see a boy spinning a top upon the floor, we can find there a typical example of the transmission of energy from one form to another. The energy which is contained in his arm is transferred to the top and it thus gyrates in a spinning motion. This spinning motion is the same energy which was but a moment before contained in the boy's arm, in cell structures and in nerve impulses. This energy must, under common physical laws, again establish itself on a certain basic equilibrium, so far as it is diametrically opposed to the physical world.

In other words, the top is now in direct conflict with at least two well-known physical laws: the principle of inertia, which means the mass of the top, as it is spinning, is in direct conflict with the rigid force or proportion of gravitational motion. There are also certain elements of friction with the molecules of air surrounding the top, as well as at the point of the top itself upon the floor and this friction in turn absorbs a certain amount of energy which was formerly in the boy's arm, turning it into what is commonly called heat.

Heat merely means that there are certain energy wave forms coming in contact with molecular structures, and in the force fields of molecules as they are compounded in compositions of atoms, the various energy wave forms in these molecular patterns are thus disturbed. The molecules can thus be said to be agitated; and in this agitation or maladjustment of their frequencies, they absorb the energy, which is heat. In the case of heat entering the human body, should this molecular maladjustment take place in such a manner and fashion that it is unable to immediately resume its normal state of equilibrium, then the person can be said to be burned upon that portion of his anatomy, as the atoms and the molecules as they were so constituted, are now not in their former normal relationship to the human body.

The foregoing principles are the common basic equivalents to many of the misconstrued scientific concepts as they relate to the stemming of heat from the sun; for in all cases we do not find either heat or any of the other so-called classifications of energy formations, as they are used in the nomenclature of the scientists. They refer purely, in their esoterical values, to the diversified transmissions and readjustments in various frequency relationships within themselves.

Energy stemming from the sun is not heat, but it comes in conjunction with the magnetic fields of the earth, such as are posed by gravitational fields as well as kinetic forces which make the earth, in effect, a very large and supercharged magnet. These energies coming from the sun are thus, through hysteresis, changed directly into such wave forms, and are altered in such manner and form that we can call them heat. This merely means that these various energy wave forms can now thus come in contact with atomic and molecular structures. In so doing, their normal pattern and their fields of force are disrupted to such an extent that they may become "heated", either largely or to a very small degree, according to the amount of energy involved in this process.

Resuming the normal course of our introspection and referring once again to the point in question—the development of an evil person as posed against the development of a good person—we must therefore understand these principles of absorption as they are concerned with the disruption of frequency patterns and relationships of various energy formations, for it is in this way that any person is developed in the superconsciousness, either as an evil or as a more positive and good person. A person can and often does develop in an evil way in the spiritual or super-consciousness, just as this same person could develop in a positive or good manner. This will account for the appearance of different external personifications of the superconsciousness as they are posed as evil or destructive forces.

For a clearer understanding of this condition, we must therefore look into the Spiritual worlds and picture for ourselves how life can and does exist for every individual when he loses his physical body. It should by now be firmly established in your mind that there is no such thing as a physical life after all and that we are all basically, internally and in any other particular way you wish to picture, actually merely expressing the common dynamics of energy transmissions as they are expressed from an infinite number of planes of consciousness which form the aggregate in correct conjunctive attitudes with positive and negative interpolations with past life experiences. Therefore, the physical life merely means that we are only expressing a common polarity in a negative fashion with the more positively biased Infinite Cos-

21

mogony.

Therefore, in the spiritual life, instead of the physical automation which has been previously described and loosely referred to as internal combustion in the human system, man will find it is, in some respects, quite similar to the life which he left in the physical world. As far as his psychic body is concerned, now that he is in the spiritual world—a creature of pure energy not living within the physical flesh—he therefore has a certain amount of spiritual aeration. Instead of the oxygen which he formerly contacted in his physical world and which made ingress into his body through his lungs, aerating his blood stream and making it possible for "combustion and metabolism" to take place to sustain life, he now has the same condition taking place in the absorption of spiritual energies directly into his psychic body from an infinite number of planes in which he now finds himself to be living. This aeration takes place again on that common basic equivalent of frequency relationship; therefore, any aeration in his psychic body must, as a natural consequence, take place in such planes of relationship which are compatible with the frequencies in his psychic body.

Thus if a person is good, this aeration will quite naturally take place in his psychic centers from planes which are constructive, or can be considered to be of a higher elevation and higher value than those being absorbed or being aerated into a person who is negatively biased and who relates this aeration process into his psychic body from such planes which are negatively biased, or which are destructively balanced against the progressive evolution of man, individually or collectively.

This process of spiritual aeration with which he is concerned in his spiritual world thus makes life possible for him and furnishes, just as food and oxygen formerly did to the physical body, the basic constituents in his spiritual development in that spiritual world. Thus it is the evil person finds just as much food and oxygen (or shall we say that we are using food and oxygen in a comparative term only), and an abundance of these negative energies to feed and nourish his psychic body as the positively biased or good person finds of the good and positive energies to aid and abet the constructive processes of his psychic body in a higher elevation.

You may wonder, therefore, and reasonably analyze that the development of the evil person could assume staggering proportions. This person could eventually develop into a similar form of an "evil" Avatar, just as is posed in the development of a "good" Avatar, and this, too, is so. We will find in these spiritual worlds there are developments, in proportion of evil persons, to a degree which is quite comparable in force and power to those who have assumed a more constructive elevation in life. However, evil does, in its own intent and purpose, always eventually destroy itself.

There is a basic reason why the development of an evil person reaches only a certain point, a point which can be considered, in modern psychological terminology, as the point of diminishing returns. In other words, in the development of this evil person as he is concerned with his superconsciousness itself, instead of becoming an outwardly expanding and constructively minded polarity with the Infinite, it becomes increasingly condensed or concentrated within itself in its evil intent and its evil purpose. Therefore, as this development—or rather should we say, this degeneration—progresses, the superconsciousness will find itself increasingly compressed and thus, in this compression, lacks accessibility to the common and general spiritual aeration which is so necessary to support and to regenerate its own purpose in the spiritual worlds.

This, in a sense of the word, means that the super-consciousness is slowly destroying itself by its own growth. This point is rather difficult for the average individual to visualize in his own mind; but it can be fully explained and justified when we have incepted the principles of relationship which involve life in the spiritual worlds. In other words, the normal progression and evolution of the Higher or the Superself does, and must always, involve an increasing number of various affiliations with what might be considered infinite planes of relationship, for it is the very nature of the superconsciousness to partake of the same infinite perspectives as the creative force which first started its evolutionary process.

We can thus say that the evil person in the material worlds, in the common relationships and in the patterns of his different lifetimes, first formed a rather highly developed Superconsciousness in a positive way. Up to a certain point, this evil person was formerly a very powerful and a very "good" person and could be compared either to an Initiate or an Adept, or perhaps even possibly a Master in his own sense, before he began to deteriorate. In the spiritual worlds, in the development of his now negatively biased Superconsciousness by the continual process of turning concept inwardly upon himself and in the revolution of the transmissions of his spiritual life as is concerned only with himself, he can thus be considered destructive. In this selfishness, he consequently compresses and degenerates his formerly developed Superconsciousness into nothingness.

CHAPTER 3

This particular concept cannot and should not be applied to the persons who are in our common existence and to whom we refer as evil. Such people have found the values of life only in such things as sex and various material attributes and they commonly express all of the very negative elements of selfishness and self-centeredness which an evil person can be considered to be expressing. It must be remembered that these people are not, in any sense of the word, developed as either spiritually "good" or spiritually "bad" people. But whenever we find a person who has formerly developed a great spiritual personality in a "good" sense and this same person has then degenerated or switched the bias, so to speak, from the direction in which his Superconsciousness has been developed, we shall find this person in dire straits and circumstances. We shall find also that this person is expressing outwardly into the physical world the sum and total of this great negation in some manner or form.

We can thus find our Hitlers, our Genghis Khans, other kings, emperors and exponents of what we might call evil forces, as they have been expressed in the pages of history. Here again is posed another question which the student may ask. It has been said that the door to reformation is never closed to any individual, and that in the more crude or primitive translations, God is all forgiving and—this is so.

Should a person at any time in this degenerative process (as he is now an evil person), find he is thus slowly destroying what he had formerly built with great care in the many lifetimes and in finding this destructive process, he can turn about and change his direction of evolution, providing of course, that he meets all of the necessary requirements as they are contained in various conjunctions, energy transmissions, concepts and other particular cycles, which are most necessary for this change-about condition. It must also be borne in mind that the evil person has multiplied infinitely the necessary amount of force which will be needed for him to change his direction. In other words, as an evil person, he has been traveling in an opposite direction through "time and space" at a tremendous rate of speed, so to speak. He can thus be compared to a man in a rocket ship who is approaching a planet and wishes to slow down the many thousands of miles an hour speed which he has attained through free space, so that he will not be burned up and destroyed by the impact with the planet which he is bent upon reaching.

The amount of energy and force necessary to change the Superconsciousness in its destructive flight and purpose, is equally proportionate to the amount of energy which was involved in constructing this Superconsciousness and projecting it in the wrong direction. It can therefore be easily conceived that this amount of energy must be tremendous and cannot be remanifested or regenerated in any one particular moment or even in one particular lifetime.

This person is now concerned with an evolutionary pattern backwards, so to speak, to backtrack his former course of evolution; he is now posed or biased in a completely positive manner, the opposite to the former one which was biased in a negative direction. This, in a sense, means that for every overt or destructive act which he has performed in his own self-ish intent and purpose, he must at least reconstruct an equally positive and diametrically opposed positive force against it in order for cancellation and catalysis to take place in this action. This process can therefore easily involve the various purgatories which have been the common belief of many people who have lived upon the planet earth, such as were described in Dante's "Inferno", and those which are preached from the pulpits of the various Christian churches. These purgatories are, quite naturally, the self-imposed conditions, as they are viewed introspectively by the individual in the spiritual worlds, as he is concerned with his own evolution. His remorse and self-recriminations are equally great and matched only by the sins and acts of his own consciousness.

This will therefore resolve the individual's own particular philosophy of life into understanding the Infinite and his own relationship to the Infinite; as the Infinite is, in itself as thus so described, Infinite. It can be conceivable, within the individual's mind, as he is posed in the various biases which are contained in his psychic body and superconsciousness that he views this Infinity in direct ratio in the common terms of frequency relationships which he has thus so far developed.

In other words, there is nothing in this Infinite Cosmogony which concerns any individual except that which he can conceive within the normal relationships and processes as they are contained in energy wave forms and patterns in the daily process and transmission of life. He will never, at any time, exceed the limits of the concepts of his own mind and, quite naturally, these concepts must be the direct result of development.

In this process of development, man gradually expands the ability of his power of concept to include a much greater proportion of the Infinite Cosmogony. When an individual has thus fully expanded his consciousness to this degree, it is imperative then, that he must also conversely, have developed the necessary determinants and attributes wherein he, as an individual, can be selective in all the proportions in which he thus is able to conceive. In other words then, he must always relate whatever proportions of Infinity he conceives within himself as constructive proportions and which are so positively biased in his own relationship of life. Should he ever, in his process of conception and lack of knowledge of this principle, inadvertently conceive and relate himself to these conceptions with Infinity, in negative wave forms—or patterns of relationship—he is thus automatically beginning his own destruction and precipitating himself in the opposite direction into the negative worlds.

This has always been the common point of departure for those who have instituted themselves as evil forces, not only in the material world but in those various astral and subastral worlds in which they function. Through the processes of life and in the determinant qualities of introspection as they concern Infinity and in their expanded and conscious state, these individuals were either not fully cognizant of, or lacked the necessary knowledge to determine these various relationships of Infinity with their own inward concepts and relationships to Infinity in a positive manner. Thus, they incurred that gradual change-about process which precipitated them into the negative direction. Another factor which abets this trend is the seeming lack of knowledge, or perhaps merely a lassitude, which could quite naturally be incurred by the individual's own false sense of proportion and power which he had assumed in his development of the superconsciousness; for a person developing to the point where he could be considered an Adept or an Avatar, could quite easily be swayed, inadvertently or otherwise, with the powers of his own Superconsciousness.

This was the problem which confronted Jesus in the Holy Land and is so graphically depicted in His temptation by the Devil on the Mount, which is only a parable in nature but illustrates the struggle which is often incurred by those who are developed in their Superconsciousness, for always this person is tempted within himself to use the power which he has developed, for his own personal gain and for his own personal development. This, as has been postulated, begins that compressive and destructive process which will eventually destroy the Superconsciousness of the individual, if it is continued in as great a proportion to that which was formerly incurred in its development.

Relationships are basically all the same and the equivalents can always be multiplied in the common terms of mathematical formulas. In other words, two times two is four; if we incur a negative force of a certain proportion and intensity and involve a certain determined amount of energy, it is quite natural to suppose it is going to take an equal amount of positive force to cancel out and neutralize this negative force, plus an added quantity of bias which would perpetuate and sustain this positive force after it has performed its operation.

Therefore, dear reader, in your new philosophy of life, you can always commonly resolve the Infinite Cosmos and your relationship to it, in regard to just how you can conceive this Infinity and just how much of this Infinity you can relate to your own particular transmission of life. In this conception, always be positively biased, for if a positive bias is not maintained, negative bias is always the penalty to pay and negative bias means eventual destruction.

As to those who have been helped or healed by some seemingly miraculous force which has been called "spiritual healing" or "divine intercession", the principles here are just the same. At the particular moment of healing, the individual has, to some small degree, learned of a certain positive bias, so far as the proportions of energy formations are posed in his psychic body, in their relationship to the Infinite. In this positively biased condition, the infinite, positive, regenerative and rebuilding power can completely reconstitute the psychic body in whatever particular malformations of negative energy with which it is so concerned. But as has been previously explained, there must also be a direct conjunction with the different functioning principles as they concern these various energy wave forms and polarity patterns which are involved in this healing process.

The average individual, in his progression of life, must destroy these old fallacious concepts, such as "divine intercession" and the belief that he can be saved from his sins and iniquities by some Master or Avatar. This is the greatest of all hypocrisies which man perpetuates not only against himself, but in teaching it to his fellow man. The adherents to this hypocrisy are always doomed to disappointment and eventual destruction should they continue their unrealistic attitude toward the Infinite Creative Force which we call God. It is the purpose of this great Infinite Creative Force to constantly perpetuate itself, re-create itself and regenerate itself in an infinite number of forms and transmissions of numerous and varied energy wave forms, whether they are of an atomic nature or whether they resolve themselves into such infinite abstractions which may be concerned with higher spiritual worlds. There is no difference; it means Infinity. The Creator is living, breathing and regenerating in all of these Infinite configurations.

The individual whose basic problem is as he is constructed—either large or small, whether atomically as in his physical body, or into the various wave forms of the psychic body—he is a part of this Infinite and as such, if he wishes to live in Infinity, he must thus become an active, participating element in this infinite process. The only reasonable and logical conclusion is that in order to be able to thus become a functioning element with this Infinity, he obviously must know something about it. He must not only know something about it but he must activate it to a much higher degree and relationship than he is now doing; and this, in itself, is the common pattern of evolution through which everyone passes in that metamorphosis which involves changing a material person into a Spiritual Being.

The material person has only begun the process of aggregation, as it concerns energy wave forms in various transmissions and purposes of life. These aggregates of energy wave forms go to make up the matrix of the negative or material ego. Thus, through evolution, in the long process of many thousands of lives and many millions of years—just as the little caterpillar undergoes the metamorphosis into a brilliantly colored butterfly—so does man, in his spiritual evolution, gradually travel into the Infinite Cosmos to become a great infinite reciprocating polarity with this Infinite Mind.

Be patient therefore, the problems of today as they concern your own relationship to this Infinite, whether they are in measures of healing as are posed against physical problems—mental or material derelictions in your daily lives mean only one thing: they are a challenge to your own personal integrity, to your strength of character as to how much you can work out in the process of daily life to offset and to correct

31

these conditions. This is the waiting process of meta-morphosis which will eventually change you from your caterpillar-like life on the earth into that radiant, brilliantly-hued spiritual person; that Avatar who will live in the future worlds.

If you have the inner knowing called faith, if you have the power and strength of character to put the necessary elements into proper operation, these things will be cancelled out in direct proportion to the amount of these divers conjunctive relationships which you put into effect at the moment. Time is of no importance but the development of the personal ego is of the utmost importance; and whether it takes 100 million years or 100 billion years, makes absolutely no difference in the eye of the Infinite Creative Force.

To you, therefore, who are groveling in your little pits of clay, look upward, for you shall find in Spirit, understanding and knowing of which Spirit is. This will be the lifting, compelling force which will elevate you from out of this pit and start you on your journey into the Infinite Cosmos.

CHAPTER 4

In his journey through life, the average and earnest truth seeker is constantly presented with a number of seeming paradoxes. The differences between political and religious systems, scientific factions, various types of social structures and ways of life, all seem to present to this person certain insoluble or incompatible differences which are very difficult to equate and which, in spite of all efforts, remain unresolved in this person's own relationship to the physical world. To the average person, this situation may or may not resolve itself as differences in these diverse ways into such various psychic pressures which may actually create a neurotic or a psychotic condition in the mind of such a person, should he try to take these differences too seriously in the transmission of his daily life.

To the truth seeker, these differences assume vast and various proportions which must be resolved and justified before evolutionary progress can be sustained in a positive direction. To say that the processes of solving these numerous differences, which are merely byproducts of time and the gradual assimilation of the various impacts of different civilizations and subsequent spiritual lives, is to follow the average evolutionary course of each individual but eventually such an individual reaches a certain threshold where the natural reactionary processes of life are not sufficient to sustain the inward spiritual drive which is contained or sustained from the superconsciousness.

When an individual reaches such a position in his evolutionary scale, he has then begun the journey which makes him ready for the complete emergence from life in the material planes as a material being (where he is subjected to the various reactionary processes of life), for this individual has become eager and longs for a life which can be more suitably equated in higher spiritual values. Some of these differences of life as are posed in the material worlds about us are contained in such seeming paradoxes existing between science and religion. While it is common knowledge that the average individual is prone to make superficial examinations of various values and to equate judgment thereon, yet such a course is fallacious. In no way or manner should any person arrive in an analysis of some difference in his daily life without taking into consideration that such things contain an infinite number of ramifications with spiritual planes in which every individual is more or less directly connected.

The scientist may, in his own way, be superficially trying (to all appearances), to destroy the whole and complete religious system by denying the existence of such supernatural phenomena as miracles and numerous other sustaining pillars of concept as they are contained in the various religious documentaries. The scientist, contrary to all appearances in this so-called destruction, is not actually so minded but is trying to prove in his own way the true, actual existence of his knowledge of the Infinite, as it is contained in the atom and in various other energy transmissions with which he is familiar. In this way, he is in some subconscious manner, relating himself to his higher superconscious self which lives in a dimension of relationship with the Infinite which has assumed some sort of a practical term of interpolation wherein he can see in mathematical equations, configurations and such other impedimenta of his scientific world, direct translations of spiritual Infinity as he knows of them in the higher moments of his lives between earth lives.

In this sense then, the scientist can actually be said to have developed somewhat further along the line of his evolution than has his religionist contemporary who is, from the pulpit or from the Bible, trying to express age-old and altered to the modern idiom of the times, various deifications as they concern the mystical forces which move about him. The religionist also is relating subconsciously into his higher self, specific knowledge and certain pertinent relationships with the higher Infinite Mind of God which he has not as yet learned to equate in mathematical formulae or into such structural forms as atoms. To this religionist, the Infinite Mind is still resolving itself into somewhat of the unknown and mystical qualities which formerly endowed it with the various propensities as it appeared in the different pantheologies and paganisms from his past lifetimes.

However, the cardinal sin (if it can be called such), which has been committed, is that in both cases— whether the scientist or the religionist—the most definite and emphatic emphasis has always been placed upon the material side of life. Both the scientist and the religionist have been trying to equate to their fellow men the whole and complete Infinite Cosmogony in terms of finite third dimensional relationships in more or less reactionary measures as they are contained either in the test tube or in the Bible. In this way too, it can be fully justified that the scientist or the religionist is still indulging in some form or another of an ancient paganism as it has been expressed in numerous past lifetimes.

The scientist has deified the atom, his mathematical formula, to the exclusion of all else; he has relegated the Infinite, so far as his exterior consciousness is concerned, into these numerous reactionary theses as are posed in his text books and which are workable in the laboratory. Likewise, the religionist is committing the same type of idolatry and cardinal sin in his expressions and translations of the Infinite Mind; for even in modern religious systems which are called Christian—but are basically pagan in nature— God is still an exterior configuration who dwells in some celestial and nebulous mansion. This is a sort of development, a white-robed Santa Claus, which has evolved from the pages of history from such ancient personages and characters as were carved in stone or cast in bronze and gold and worshiped by the multitudes.

This is in direct contradiction to the context of the gospel as it was preached by Jesus of Galilee, in which Jesus stressed so emphatically—and which fortunately has not been deleted from modern biblical translations—that the all-important concept to the individual is his relationship with the Infinite. It is all concept and must take place from within the individual himself and not from some exterior or some superficial values which may be posed in his immediate environment. This then, is the threshold of true spiritual expansion. It is the point or the beginning, which Buddha called Nirvana, in which the existence of the soul of man can be fully justified as living in spiritual dimensions without the seemingly necessary vehicle of the human body.

In this way then, basically, whether scientist or religionist or those who are more or less sitting across the fence and might in common terminology be called atheists but, large or small, whatever may be their particular relationship to this life, as long as they remain materialists and try to resolve the common equations of the Infinite Mind into common equivalents of reactionary values in their daily life, they can be considered paganistic in their attitude of life; and as such, they are indulging in the age-old evolutionary pattern of life which can be referred to as idolatry.

People today, in our modern world, are just as paganistic in nature as they were thousands of years ago except, of course, their idolatry has taken on new and more modern forms of expressions. We find idolatry, or worship to the exclusion of the higher spiritual values, appearing on the surface of life in many different forms and ways, whether it is in the worship of new automobiles, home furnishings, or bedecking the person with new clothes, mink stoles or whatever particular type of idolatry we may see in these various expressions of life about us. Too, the teenager has his own particular type of idolatry, just as does the more mature advanced person. No one, old or young, male or female is completely immune to these various forms of idolatry as they sweep about us expressing themselves in our daily lives.

The churchgoer is just as guilty of idolatry as were the Israelites who bowed down to worship the golden calf when Moses was on Mount Sinai. Likewise is the man or woman who makes the art of making money his daily fetish; their sum and total of daily insecureities, as they are posed from various negative subconscious inflictions, makes an aggregate of various negative indispositions which culminate in a frenzied, frantic scramble for the so-called necessities of life. This, in itself, poses one of the greatest of all paradoxes, for in the Infinite Cosmos there is an abundance of everything. Each person, individually can, on the basis of introspection, look infinitesimally small and be much less than the common atoms of which his body is composed. Therefore, living in this infinite sea

37

of energy which pulsates, radiates and vibrates about him in this superabundant cosmogony with an abundance of everything which man needs for his daily life—he is constricted in his pattern of life by this mad scramble for survival.

This too, in its modern form, is simply an evolution in which possibly the same man who is now sitting in the swivel chair of a banker's office was just a few thousand years ago, a primitive savage with a stone axe stalking his prey through the jungle. While conditions and manners of expression have greatly changed, the basic principle for survival is still the ulterior motive in all of his daily actions and, altruistically speaking, the higher motivating spiritual values have finally vaguely begun to manifest themselves into his spiritual life in such a manner and form that he will drop a dollar bill on the plate in his church.

Who can say, then, in viewing the race of mankind, existing on the earth today, that even in his most advanced form of living, he is not the much vaunted and developed creature which he presupposes himself to be. His bump of approbation must constantly be massaged with daily applications of ego-salve which he administers to himself in order that he may survive and re-inflict the burden of his karmic existence from one day to the next.

From all corners of the land, all ways and reaches on the earth's surface comes the inharmonious, blatant bleat of the multitudes in their various sins and iniquities, crying out for relief, for salvation and for some basic equivalent of security in their seemingly insecure world and in the existence in which they live. People who basically have not yet developed beyond the age of childhood and who daily express themselves in such common relationships which are quite childlike and elemental in nature, strangely enough have become the focusing point of certain systems of idolatries which are practiced in the world today.

We see for instance, in our American way of life and in the entertainment world, people who would, in the ordinary manner and way of life, remain totally unknown, for basically they are people with little, if any, talent beyond the ordinary values of what might be called the expressive way of life. These people clutter up the airwaves of the different electronic devices, such as radio, television and the theater with their blatant and nefarious portrayals of the various emotional and reactionary ways of life. In this way, sex is the predominating influence which is expressed in all of these various entertainment portrayals. Second but by no means lagging very far behind, is the old destructive attitude of life which has portrayed itself in many of the bloodiest pages of history— the destruction of one man by another—for murder rides hand in glove with sex down the air-lanes and throughout the various halls of portrayal in our entertainment world.

Here we find the craven cowards enjoying these different expressions; these cowards of their own selves, people who are still living in the fears, the haunts, the insecurities of their former lives; the shadows of the images of people they have killed, destroyed, looted and plundered in former times are still stalking the hallways of their memories. Then too, because of certain law enforcement systems, these people who would otherwise be quite prone to go out and practice their various nefarious affiliations with past lives have now, by common sense, been restrained from so doing because they know that this would inevitably bring about a complete cessation of their lifetime activities. This also adds to the burden of pressure as it is posed in their various psychic centers relating to these different expressions of past lives. It is quite natural therefore, that these people should at least seek some sort of a palliative to relieve these pressures. This they can do by finding in their common entertainment world, an expression wherein people publicly, legally and lawfully can portray to their patronage the destructive arts which have been banned from those who are viewing them.

Here again in our objectivism, this condition carries a fair measure of warning. The old cliché that "like begets like" is based upon our understanding of frequency relationships. As Jesus expressed it, "Bread cast upon the waters returns tenfold." And again we have that common understanding of frequency relationship and the combination of harmonic creation.

Chapter 5

To express a good and constructive thought, whether or not it is followed by an action, means this good and constructive thought, as a definite wave form, has behind it the potential of consciousness and is psychokinetically projected into the Infinite Cosmos. There, in frequency relationship, it finds an infinite number of wave forms which are compatible to it in nature and also good in nature which can be considered constructive. Therefore this thought regenerates a certain harmonic structure which, in turn through cyclic patterns, regenerates itself on the surface of the life of the individual who first cast the good and constructive thought into the ethers.

This same principle holds true of people who cast negative thoughts into the Infinite; and here is a measure of warning: thought without action is just as potent as if the action had been committed. To commit adultery mentally is just as much of a sin as actually to perpetrate the sin in a physical sense; the idea behind all such manifestations is that these things usually enslave the perpetrator to the exclusion of all constructive ideologies, forms and manifestations. Here again we find that common linkage through frequency relationship, not only to the Infinite Cosmos but to an infinite number of people who are or who have committed such nefarious or negative relationships in their life.

These negative thoughts, in turn, will regenerate those harmonic structures which are ever increasingly negative in nature and which, through cyclic patterns and frequency relationship, will regenerate themselves on the surface of the life of the individual who first cast them into the Infinite. Thus we see the beginning of both a spiritually good person and a very vile or evil person and it can truly be said to be the beginning, or the end.

The average individual on the face of the earth who is neither so negatively biased nor positively biased that he expresses a preponderance of either one or the other of these relationships in his daily life is not lost, nor is he without cause. This person, if given all the benefit of the doubt, will usually evolve after millions of years into a constructively minded participating element in the Infinite Cosmogony. For the present then, we can look upon him and easily justify and forgive him in whatever particular transgressions he may be committing against our sense of decency and justice. We can overlook his beer, his sex and his cigarettes, his selfishness, his grasping attitudes and know, in the development of the Superego Consciousness, he will attain that metamorphosis in the future eons of time; providing of course, that some particular affiliation or a preponderance of negative force does not turn the direction of his progress from the upward to the downward trail.

To each one, therefore who is a truth seeker, may we say, do not lose sight of the fact that you will be forever tempted with the preponderance of false values as they are posed in your own relationship to yourself. Jesus was tempted by the "devil" in the parable in the New Testament; but factually speaking, this temptation actually existed with this Master for many hundreds, or possibly many thousands of years. It was a daily temptation to be reckoned with constantly and necessitated Jesus living in constant alertness and vigilance so at no time would He be committing an act which could be justified as being selfish in nature. After learning of Spiritual Wisdom, if He had used the great powers which were his for his own selfish purpose, He would have automatically, and at that moment, turned his flight and progression from the upward to the downward path.

The false systems of various idolatries as we find them about us in the world today, are very serious defects in the transmission of our way of life in the various levels of social structures in which we find ourselves, for idolatries and various idols always have the same nefarious and undermining effect upon the spiritual anatomy of the Superconsciousness. In the oscillating process, as it is concerned with the exterior surface of a person's life and with the interior or the psychic self, as it has lived in other lifetimes, unless these things are constantly and positively biased in complete spiritual retrospection, analogously, these various oscillations can then be considered negative in nature and, as such, destructive. They can also be called systems of idolatry; for idols always have a tendency to focus the consciousness of the person from the interior to the exterior. It is this exterior world, the world of reaction with which the person is basically involved in leaving behind, in his upward flight into the Infinite.

Be not afraid, therefore, to substitute higher spiritual values for what might seem, at the moment, to be apparent substantial physical values of relationship even though the exchange of the higher spiritual concepts seem, in a sense or at that moment, to have no supporting means nor even to have a functional relationship. But in all cases, such particular relationships and their subsequent substitutions will, in future evolutions of time, come to mean the actual difference between constructive evolution and a downward plunge into the abysmal reaches of the subastral worlds.

The reactionists, the scientists and the religionists who cannot or who do not translate their way of life and that of their fellow men into the elements of life which are directly connected in a scientific and fully justified manner with the Infinite, are hopelessly lost within themselves until such junctions with this Infinite Consciousness can be constructively maintained on the surface of their future lives. This is also part of the age-old escape mechanism of spiritual healing, the long-dreamed-of and nebulous equation of a perfect way of life; the Utopia, the Shangri-La, where sin and evil and all the various deleterious factions of life have been removed by some great spiritual faction or leadership.

Such a condition is contrary to a true way of life and at no time is any individual in such a position that he is not immediately confronted with all of the infinite problems and relationships of life as they are concerned in direct translations with his immediate life, for to be thus suspended and taken away from want and insecurity would in itself violate the most hallowed precincts of our evolutionary pattern of life, completely destroying the prime purpose of the creation of man and his relationship to the Creator.

Life therefore can and always should be visualized as a constructive evaluation of equations in an infinite number of relationships. Primarily, all this must be by reason of the way, manner and form in which it is lived. For its creation is basically and essentially energy, or spiritual in nature. Therefore, man must always if he is so constructively minded—live his pattern and transmission of life from a spiritually minded platform wherein he understands, to some degree, the numerous translations of life as they relate to energy wave forms, in that constructive and evolutionary process of the psychic body in conjunction with the Higher Self.

To cry out to Jesus or to any spiritual healer, self-constituted or otherwise, is only a direct reversion into ancient paganisms and savage or barbaric customs, wherein some witch doctor or purveyor of so-called mystical powers was purveyed for a fee to the general public who so demanded his services. In the back reaches of the jungles today, we see savages wearing about their necks, different charms which are concocted of weird and varied forms of animal and vegetable life; their sole virtue lies only in the fact the wearer believes in them. The same system of idolatry is today contained and personified in many ways in our social structures. Perhaps so far as the religionist is concerned, he is wearing his Bible about his neck, just as the savage in the jungle wears his feathers and lion's claws about his neck. These things largely have been only developments and new adaptations of old forms and expressions.

So, dear brother, if you find yourself in stringent circumstances—financial, physical, mental or otherwise—remember these things, in themselves, are all a direct result of your own creation. You spent thousands of years erecting this little wall of false ideas, associations and translations about you so you now find yourself almost isolated from the Infinite Cosmogony. There is only one way to climb over this wall; to realize that it is within yourself and only you have the power to do so. In conjunction with the various spiritual attributes which you have acquired in your evolution and in the development of the Superconsciousness, this could be a veritable bolt of lightning descending from heaven and, in one fell stroke, level that little wall you have erected around yourself. You would then find yourself freed from the trammel, the toil and the vicissitudes of the material implications in which you have so confounded yourself. This sav-

45

ing Master, who so precipitated this great bolt, was the sum and total of all the good things which you had learned and compared, evaluated and equated, interwoven, polarized and biased and which so positively-minded you from your spiritual side of life.

Look not, therefore, for your healing in the church, the temple or in the hospital. Your healing will come about directly after certain particular justifications have been made with the exterior surface of your life, called the physical, to the various interpolations of consciousness as they are contained in the Superconsciousness which, in turn, oscillates infinitely into that constructive Infinite Mind which has been called God.

PART TWO

CHAPTER 6

In his search for Truth and at different points in some particular lifetime (and we could consider the present life as an example), the average truth seeker may find himself more directly concerned with the outside world and the multitudes of people who inhabit these different countries with which he is connected. By some particular rapport with the Inner Consciousness, he has been quickened or alerted to higher spiritual values and these spiritual values, the knowledge of and the living in the spiritual worlds, have become a closer relationship to him.

These things in themselves pose many and varied contrasts; some, very striking in nature with the outside world in which he lives. He may thus become acutely aware of the various derelictions, suffering and other particular types of life which can be basically animalistic or reactionary in nature. Thus quickened or sensitized in seeing these varied contrasts, he may immediately wish in some way or manner to change the whole contour of the existing world. This may even be aided and abetted, in a sense, by a psychological equivalent known as an escape mechanism.

The sum and total of the various psychic pressures which are oscillating in his psychic self, as they are so concerned and connected with negative indispositions of a destructive nature with past lifetimes, along with this particular quickening (as he is now so spiritually posed), only tend in a way to aid or to further the urgency of his need to see his fellow men changed in their seemingly mad rush to oblivion.

In this way he accomplishes a twofold purpose: he can justify, to some degree (or he believes he can), the various spiritual beliefs and knowledge which he has acquired in higher worlds. He can also divert his attention subconsciously from the sense of his own guilts and iniquities. In this way, that particular individual often becomes quite unreasonable and even fanatical in his expression of life. He may find common union in such cultisms and various other religious expressions which are primarily motivated by the more fanatical expressions concerning man's interpolations of his daily life. Yes, it is not impossible to find in various churches of the country today, as well as in other religious systems existing in other lands, some very strange and weird customs which are always engendered by this common escape mechanism and the added quickening of the spirit to the higher sense of spiritual values.

This person, either mildly or fanatically inclined to change the world, can become a real menace not only to himself but to everyone with whom he comes in contact. Not only is he prone to exaggerate the position of the world as it presently exists, but quite often the propaganda which he spreads finds sympathetic ears in people who have reached a common borderline but have not yet crossed into that nebulous threshold in which the fanatic is now revolving. This fanatical person will therefore find various and obtrusive manners and forms in which he can express the fanaticism and the escape from reality into some direction which completely detracts from his true constructive evolutionary course.

We will find today, in this modern world, people who are worshiping in strange rituals not only such things as snakes and other forms of animal or vegetable life, but people who chase flying saucers and worship at the altars of the various movie idols in the entertainment world. These things, in themselves, can always be considered diversionary methods or manners of expression in the common escape mechanism. In the fanatic who assumes the religious role of a purveyor of a great truth, we again find a menace of a different sort and one which should be reckoned with. Should this fanatic be so obsessed that he can gather about him—either consciously or otherwise— a supporting band of astral entities, as is so often the case, who are also so fanatically inclined, through the subconscious reaches and in frequency relationship, they will often exert outwardly into the physical of that man's life a very strange and hypnotic influence which will reach into the lives and conduct of many people whom he contacts.

We shall thus see the reason why people meekly or even hypnotically follow the leadership of some person who is obviously a psychopath in every sense, manner and form; who is obsessed not only with the idea of changing the way and manner of his followers, but also with the dethroning of every known precinct of consciousness in our social structures. Neither can it be said that these fanatics have any real or basic supporting platforms which could, in any sense of the word, give a new world or a justified reason for the change of manners or customs in the people whom

49

they do contact. Usually these fanatics are quite barren in their own lives and upon close scrutiny will be found to possess feet of clay and who are, at the present time, standing upon pedestals of their own erection.

When Jesus said, "By their fruits ye shall know them," He gave us a sort of slide rule or a common denominator wherein we could, in all phases and concepts of life, truly measure the worth of any particular one of our expressionary values. This one in particular was concerned with the spiritual values. It was of the utmost importance that we should find this fruit would yield large and abundant returns in a manner and form which could change the way and manner of life for one or many individuals—not in some fanatical and unrealistic pursuit of some miasmic or mesmeric form or some cultism which leads a person down the primrose trail to oblivion—but real transforming elements in this person's life which would not only dissolve the confusion in his mind but actually clear away his physical difficulties as they existed in the body. Such fruit is indeed hard to find; and again, a close examination of our various religious systems in the world will find the ground is very sterile and barren. There are few, if any, trees which bear fruit.

Yes, we can include even such particular evangelistic movements which are supposed to have had great healing influences upon certain particular thousands of adherents who have clung tenaciously to the skirts and robes of these factions. They have hung up their crutches and braces in the foyer of the temple wherein they worshiped at this false idol, when the truth of the matter was that here again they found only a certain conjunction of energy relationships which started a ringing action and a direct rapport into the higher psychic centers which enabled those persons to remove themselves from the obsessive relationships of karmic experiences. It should always be remembered when following one of these fanatics and so-called faith healers, that while you are looking hypnotically into his eyes, he will quite likely have his hand in your pocket while he is so mesmerizing the intent and purpose of your life. Thus you can be completely diverted from the natural and constructive evolution in your progress.

Nor can we fail to consider the practitioners as they are concerned in the various cults and religious systems. They are practicing their so-called healing arts at great expense to the public, for we shall find them also in doctors' offices here and there and wherever we go in this world about us. In this sense of the word, it can be said that this is an outgrowth of the natural desire of every man to dominate another. The old law of the survival of the fittest, as posed by Darwin, has been in a sense greatly overworked and has gone far beyond the bounds from which it was originally intended by the Infinite Creator, to substantiate or to increase the propensities of some particular species of animal life. When it begins to involve propensities which can be considered vampirish in nature, that is, preying upon the souls of our fellow men, then we must of course draw the line. The astral underworlds are full of the adherents of these religious fanatics; each in turn is, in common relationship, trying very diligently in any manner and form to perpetuate his false fanaticism in whatever way and manner he can into the material world.

It can be said at this time, the fanatic is very easy to recognize. The first criterion is of course, to closely examine his life and that of his adherents and if there is any real and constructive fruit which has been born, then it could be said that this fanatic has at least some virtue in his expression. However, with a true fanatic, such virtue is extremely rare and difficult to find and lies, whenever so found, within the very nature and virtue of the adherents themselves. Many of his followers may be people who are more advanced spiritually or, at least not so preconditioned and deviated with escape mechanisms and have still been able to reach through these miasmic energy forms and maintain some sort of a constructive relationship with the Higher Self, thus correcting their own difficulties and the practitioner or the fanatic usually gets the credit.

A second evaluation of all such divers components of humanitarian efforts can be analyzed on the basis of constructive, intelligent progression, not only in the various values of the reactionary life in which man finds himself, but especially into such spiritual values as are so strangely missing from the numerous pantheologies as they exist today. While man is basically and essentially a spiritual creation and always functions from a spiritual plane of relationship, yet this in itself is the greatest of all paradoxes, for by far, the greatest number of people who swarm the face of the earth do not seem to know the first rudimentary equivalents of this progressive cycle which is called life.

Here again we have found reversions and sterilizations in spiritual principles among our so-called Christians for the very pagans they try to teach are quite often further advanced in their knowledge of the spiritual worlds than the Christians who are supposedly bringing them the new and only Gospel. So, then you may ask, how is humanity to be changed in this particular time and place? Are we all headed down that trail and over the precipice to oblivion? Are any of the other various and sundry fears and calamities —atomic explosions and world-wide destructions— to be realized, or shall the old prophecies of the Bible

52

such as are contained in the Epistle of Peter, come to pass? These things should not be answered with a yes or a no because any particular position in which an individual finds himself so contained collectively regarding the masses of people about him, represents a very definite point on his scale of evolution.

CHAPTER 7

One thing which all people have in common is an abnormal sense or fear of death; and here again is the strange paradox, for in the sleeping and waking state, man dies and relives at least once every 24 hours. Yet, the word death which is actually only a Latin word meaning change, strikes terror into the heart of the materialist. Even the religionist who inhabits the church is filled with dreads, fears and vagaries. No one seems to be at that particular point in his expression of life where he can see the continuity of expression as he so lives it at any particular moment for he is directly connected through frequency relationship with at least a thousand lifetimes lived in the past. He has discarded his body at various intervals (as it is connected with that particular life), to be reborn and again live in the future in almost the identical circumstances, following the same thought patterns and obeying the same psychic impulses as motivated him in his former lives.

To study statistics as they present themselves in this present-day modern world, does indeed give everyone a sense of dread or foreboding. When we can study the high rate of incidence in the various hospitals, asylums and, in particular, the mental status quo of John Q. Citizen as he inhabits our civilized world today, these statistics do indeed indicate grave conditions.

As in all cases and in normal sequences, evolution can always be largely envisioned as a progressive cycle, but understanding the structural qualities, the movement of these cyclic forms and the energy forms from which they are so constructed, you are immediately reminded that here again is our common equivalent in polarity patterns; there is always a positive and a negative. We must also resort back into history and find man has always lived, to some degree, in these cyclic patterns of progression and retrogression.

For instance, for about 1500 years the people of the eastern world throughout Europe, lived under a completely false doctrine of physiology as it was first instigated by a man called Galen, who lived at the beginning of the Christian era. Galen did not know about the circulation of the blood or about various other functions of the anatomy yet people often died as a direct result of opposing these false doctrines.

In the Middle Ages of Europe, there appeared a complete revision of these false principles of anatomy as they were thus supposed to exist. As a result of the pursuits of certain dedicated souls, through dissection, a vast knowledge of anatomy was finally brought into existence, often at the expense of the lives of these various devoted exponents of medical truth as they found it in their various explorations. Therefore, we cannot presuppose at this time that any medical system as it presently exists can solve any or all of the differences in the physical world in which we find ourselves.

Today medical science is struggling in a maze of paradoxes, just as is every other particular faction existing on the face of the earth. To an almost total degree, medical science does not have a complete answer for either the true cause or the originating source of many of the hundreds of incurable diseases with which it is presently confronted. Medical science is therefore, at least for the present, relegated to a highly developed system of physical diagnoses, and the removal of certain offending organs or portions of the body which have broken down because of numerous and varied psychic pressures from the past.

The equivalent of medical science, our modern psychiatry is also singularly devoid of any spiritual values which relate man either to his higher self or to his past lives. Freud completely divested mankind of his so-called instincts, with the exception of one which is sex. Carl Jung added (and very boldly), a second which is gregarity. Yet neither one of these psychologists knew what an instinct was simply because they had not related (at least publicly), any knowledge which they may have inwardly known, relating man to his past lives.

Actually, in a sense, there is no such thing as an instinct. An instinct, in itself, is merely an energy wave form which is stemming constantly in an oscillating manner out from the psychic body and which is, in its vortical pattern, formed there in a former lifetime or in a number of former lifetimes.

Thus medical and psychiatric sciences, as they exist today, do not have the solution to the so-called incurable diseases. Looking as they do upon the exterior or the physical, they make the common universal mistake (so far as the material man is concerned), of trying to evaluate the whole Infinite Cosmogony by a certain number of reactionary occurrences which have thus appeared upon the surface of life. People today are thus hopelessly incarcerated as insane, or are dying from incurable diseases, or are diverted and thwarted from a normal expression of life through the sheer ignorance of those who have authority over them and who are upon the pedestals which they have erected for themselves in the medical and psychiatric fields; yes, even in the pulpits of the churches.

In His mission in the Holy Land 2000 years ago, Jesus gave a certain basic concept which, if and when it is carried through by the individual, will free him from these various dogmatic and death-dealing systems as they are found in the material world. This was the concept contained in the expression, "Seek ye the kingdom of Heaven which is within." When this concept is resolved into constituents which are understandable by the average person, it will mean simply that this person is only the sum and total of what he can conceive in his own mind; and these conditions, existing as energy wave forms, will automatically link him to either the subversive elements of the astral worlds—with all their sins, iniquities and purgatories—or they will conversely link him to the higher spiritual planes and freedom. He, in finding that freedom, will be in a position from which he can reciprocate and oscillate with the Infinite.

CHAPTER 8

Just as was prophesied in the Bible, that in the latter days there would be many false teachers and false prophets, our systems of idolatry have indeed fully justified this prophecy. However, people can be considered largely responsible, to a certain degree, for many of the false gods and teachers who they find about them in their world today.

They are continually supporting false political systems which breathe, like the fiery dragons of old, the fires of war, hell, hate and destruction of their fellow men. While even on bended knee, they beseech their god to lead them to victory over their fellow men with the sword and gun. Nor is that particular custom any different from that of the pagan in the many past lifetimes of which these people were a part at that particular time. One of the most common practices in which man has indulged throughout the various periods of history and time and which has been depicted on temple walls and in historical documentaries, are the constant prayers and pleas to the various ruling and dominating spiritual forces or gods, to lead them to victory while beheading their fellow men.

Today, men sit at a great "peace table", united, nation to nation and rubbing elbows with each other while supposedly threshing out the common problems of international differences; yet the fires of war burn fiercely in many countries. Interracial hatred is a vile virus which has swept over the face of the earth and the Four Horsemen of the Apocalypse ride ramp-

ant and roughshod over the civilizations of m.
To the truth seeker who is personally concern
the world about him and with his position to i
things can be fully compromised only when it ᵼᵤ ᵣe-
membered in his own mind and in his relationship
to the Infinite, that this condition is a very necessary
part in the evolution of every individual. It can be
likened somewhat to the smelting of the iron ore into
some useful article which will help man overcome
some particular physical difference in the world
about him.

The millions of souls who have come and gone
upon this material planet and who are so linked to it
with these psychic bonds through reincarnation, are,
in themselves, finding just as we all have, the various
additives and the condiments of various spiritual
values in the translations and transmissions of energy wave forms as they go to make up our psychic
bodies. To be directly concerned with these things in
a negative fashion will mean, as has been previously
postulated, to create direct linkage to certain reverb-
eratory actions which take place. Therefore, it behoo-
ves all constructively minded seekers to approach a
realistic philosophy in their evaluation of the position
of their fellow men and this should be done with
introspection and with positive bias.

The pits of clay which have been dug by the multitudes are quite necessary for them to live in at the
present time. They are not much further along in their
scale of evolution than they were when they dug
themselves burrows in the sides of the hills or even
wove themselves little cocoons before emerging into
the butterfly state. The sum and total of the different
values which they are expressing into their physical
lives are aggregates and collections of previous lives
which have been found and expressed in numerous
elevations of life. These aggregates live and are per-

petuated from life to life as a definite collection of personality quotients called, in modern psychological parlance, the "ego", "eto", "id", etc.

How then, in view of this light and knowledge, could anyone be deprived of these common instincts when even the function of breathing is an age-old custom—a habit man acquired through evolution? How then, according to genetical science, could all of the constituents of immortality be perpetuated in the chromosomes and genes as they were transferred from male to female? For these are but atomic structures and, in themselves, serve only as a channel and a purpose for the psychic self to regenerate into the physical form, all of the thought patterns of conciousness which formerly supported it in a previous life.

To make a sum and total of evaluations at the present moment would indeed be a herculean task; one not necessarily so contrived that it would serve the individual as a purpose to solve all his differences, for this, too, is an evolutionary pattern of progress. Sufficient to say, therefore, do not be too concerned with your own personal position, either physically or otherwise at the present moment, for you have indeed a greater proportion, a greater equilibrium of spiritual values which you have not as yet called upon or used in this material world and which would not only completely offset these differences but could re-create for you a much better pattern of life.

This immediate present, as you are thus so concerned, will be dissolved when full realization, in your future evolutions, can be thus connected and established within the precincts of your own consciousness. In this way, too, will come a proper evaluation —a relationship with the world about you and it will no longer indulge itself into such fanaticisms and expressions of life which are so commonly found. Nor will you be prone to indulge yourself in various systems of idolatry. Instead you will find inwardly, through the reaches of your own inner self, the peace, the complacency, the necessary spiritual impetus or drive and all of the necessary ingredients and components which go to make up a life which can be said to be a life of peace and proper relationship with the Infinite; and one in which you have placed yourself upon a proper evolutionary path onto that spiraling pathway to the stars.

CHAPTER 9

In the foregoing texts, the reader may now have arrived at some definite points of equation wherein he has established within his mind, that considerable importance has been stressed into specific areas of these various configurations in his position to the Infinite. In one respect, the term Infinite itself can be considered of the utmost importance. The term Superconsciousness also may indeed at this point, present certain aspects which are not at present fully apparent in the reader's interpolation. Therefore, we shall approach this subject and its context by stating that the much confused term God, or gods, as posed in numerous cultisms, religions and texts in past dispensations of mankind throughout his existence on the planet earth, can and should be resolved into this one common equation: there is indeed no personal relationship or personal deification involved in the relationship of the Infinite to man as the Infinite is, in all aspects, just as it should be thoroughly understood—Infinite.

This means that so far as space is concerned in the understanding of the modern scientist, his belief is a complete delusion. If we could conceive in the conscious mind for an instantaneous moment, the completion of the Infinite, we would find that space is infinitely filled, infinitely hard, so far as consciousness was reactive to it. In this sense therefore, so far as the material dimension is concerned, the term resistance is of the utmost importance, for all known physical laws function from the plane of reactance or resistance. The two words or terms are synonymous in their exact proportion as far as personal identities or interpolations of science are concerned, whether they relate to any expression, as is commonly composed in diametrically opposed forces of gravity, inertia, centripetal or centrifugal forces. These are all common derivatives of reactance or resistance in their various compounded infractions in the materialistic dimension of atomic forms.

The Infinite therefore must not be divided in any symposium of compounded infractions of atomic forms, but must assume proportions wherein we can see that the so-called space is actually a completely, infinitely filled solid. So far as our proportions of introspection are concerned in traveling through space, means that consciousness at any given time, interprets only a very small fraction of this infinitely filled space in terms of resistance or reactance. Thus, these various reactive factors, as they are so presently concerned with consciousness, are to the then existing concepts, the only existing and tangible elements of the Infinite; this then explains the common fallacy from which all present dispensations of materialistic sciences are so compounded.

The Infinite can therefore be said to exist in an infinite number of ways; and as has been previously postulated, as the Infinite is energy, that energy moves as it does in complete compatibility within itself as an oscillating motion concerned in a cyclic pattern. These energy wave forms can be either compatible in the relationship of vibration—as they are combined with each other—or they can also be completely or diametrically opposed to each other. We then can reason that such differences must therefore be divided into what is commonly referred to as a dimension, wherein we shall find a large number of suitably vibrating or harmonic wave form structures in cyclic paths, which are resonating in certain common basic fundamental relationships. As such, in these relationships, they are transferring to and from each other, the common idiom of that particular dimension so far as its own intelligence is concerned.

Dimensions are subsequently, in scientific parlance, subdivided into such other existing combinations of basic structures (called spectrums), such as light, heat and sound. The physical body and the five senses involved in sustaining the physical body on the planet earth, are all involved with these various subdivisions of spectro energies in their reactive or resistive forces against these five senses.

To approach more thoroughly the concept of the Superconsciousness—as has been postulated from the beginning of Christianity and taught by Jesus— such compounds of intelligence as are found in various infinite symposiums which relate to the Infinite, can therefore be subtracted and evaluated on a more understandable basis. To look into the Infinite, therefore, we shall find that in different forms and posing as aggregates of sympathetic vibrations, certain confluxes of energy are thus compatibly inclined to separate themselves into similar interdimensional forms of relationships. These aggregates thus gather together in nuclear forms, wherein certain species of plant or animal life are constantly repropagated into some specific form upon the planet earth.

As a direct result of oscillating outwardly—as intelligence is impounded inwardly—these various nuclei or cell structures, in a spiritual sense, are thus expressing themselves in such species or forms of plant and animal life; and here again we shall find a larger development of these specific cells or nuclei. In attaining a fuller measure of this development, the species of Homo sapiens, or man, thus begins an evolutionary journey through many lifetimes upon planets similar to the planet earth.

Here again are the cell-like spiritual structures, as they are compounded from such aggregates of past lifetimes. In the symposiums of these numerous and infinite aggregates which have been oscillating compounds from infractions of past animal life species upon the face of the earth, man will, in direct consequence so far as the individual is concerned, express the various relative constituents of these numerous evolutionary forms as they are so compounded. This will explain why man has a pair of lungs which aerate the blood stream and various other organs which are necessary (or so he thinks), in conjunctive form with the so-called subconscious to sustain his life which he values very highly.

This does not, in any sense of the word, relate man to a form of higher consciousness which we have stressed as the Superconsciousness. The Superconsciousness relates in a more positive dimensional form, certain aggregates of the Infinite Mind, which in the term Infinite, means there is a direct finite creative purpose in all forms of consciousness. The aggregates of the finite consciousness—as they are posed in the Infinite Mind—also form the same basic spiritual cell structures or nuclei which relate to all the positive essences, not only of earth-life existences as they are compounded in all forms and manners of species of life upon the earth, but also compounded in an infinite manner from all extractions of future lifetimes wherein these different nuclei or cell structures of spiritual energy will evolve into higher states of consciousness.

Herein enters a great principle; that again, through compatible frequency relationships as they are composed from these infinite cell structures in the Superconsciousness, they are oscillating or reflecting outwardly into the material dimensions. Thus they are controlling, through frequency relationships, the various aggregate forms of life as they are found in a suitable and compatible system of relationships. This, then, is the Superconsciousness, or the cell of life which is the aggregate—the sum and total of all of the infinite forms of consciousness which can be called the Infinite Mind. We are not concerned at the present moment with the origin of the Infinite Mind as it expresses itself infinitely, for this would indeed be far beyond the reach of any present mental consciousness. Sufficient to say, however, that even as we know Infinity in the present tense, it is only a small fraction or a small group of compounds of an over-all Infinity which would indeed stagger the imagination.

The Superconsciousness, then, can be pictured as a sort of vortex; as a cell wherein an infinite number of wave forms which, in their oscillation, present to Infinity the sum and total of all its aggregates. Thus this re-creative process, as has been described, constantly reflects and relates itself into an infinite number of other dimensions of relationship. This then, in conjunction with the previously described cell of life as it evolves and aggregates itself from various physical interpolations, becomes that particular sustaining part of the life consciousness which is called the ego.

The ego is not in any sense of the word to be confused with the Freudian concept which relates merely to extractions of the subconscious reactionary senses and interpolations of many different reactionary experiences of the past. But, in this common terminology, we are relating the ego to the spiritual form and substance as a finite form of consciousness and oscillating in direct conjunction with the Infinite.

It can also be pictured that this conjunctive oscillation with the Higher Self, or the Superconsciousness, is the sustaining life force, or the libido which gives the necessary impetus to sustain life through the numerous physical as well as spiritual dimensions. Thus it can be considered the Guiding Light, or the motivating force behind all life actions as they are concerned individually or collectively with mankind. In this broad sense, therefore, it can be said that any man, whether he is prince, pauper, beggar, merchant or thief is equally important in the Eyes of Infinite Consciousness for he is reflecting or expressing only for the moment—in whatever position he finds himself upon such a planet as the earth or in some other astral dimension—the part of Infinity as it was originally compounded in the Superconsciousness.

This concept may seemingly compose within itself certain opposing doctrines of good and evil as they are so commonly accepted throughout the infinite number of interpolations of mankind upon the planet earth. The old struggle of good and evil is a primeval cause and sprang from out of the more primitive reaches of man's consciousness upon the earth. Such forces as good and evil always were and must always remain, merely as compounds of relatively misunderstood forces which move about man in the cosmic ethers. Referring to such terms as cosmic ethers, we are again referring to that seeming void which is actually an infinitely filled solid.

Therefore, good and evil must be properly understood; that whatever our position in respect to any movement of Infinity—which it is going through in our so-called dimension of time and space—merely means that in our interpretation of this movement of intelligence, as it is either diametrically opposed to or is moving with our present conjunctive position with the Infinite, is the determinant element in that which we term good and evil but has no meaning in the personal equivalent so far as Infinite Consciousness is concerned. Good and evil can therefore be considered, in common abstractions, as the sum and total of the Infinite Mind and when thoroughly understood, will present to the reader his first important step in his own evolution to destroy the old illusions of good and evil as they have been compounded from such infractions of various pantheologies and cultisms in previous lifetimes. These illusions will be replaced by more basic and fundamental concepts of the Infinite and as these relationships of intelligence move in this seemingly voidless void about him, it remains with each individual to properly relate such movements and interpret them into constructive evaluations and patterns in his own evolution.

After the reader or the student has made this first basic and important step, he will have passed over the threshold of the old carnal or lustful world and the many implications of good and evil which it has formerly held for him. Instead, Infinity will present to him a never-ending succession of new fabrications and various contexts which he is able to extract from his forward evolution into this timeless and spaceless Infinite.

CHAPTER 10

The reader must remember that time and space are synonymous in all respects, for if we did not have time, we would not have space. Time and space means only the transference, in some specific relationship of an idea or form of consciousness from one plane of equation to another. The sum and total of all intelligence as posed in the Infinite Consciousness, is therefore, in direct terms of frequency relationship—space. These confusing elements of time can be eliminated, for the existence of this consciousness in any form merely means that it relates itself in frequency relationship to various existing compatible relationships in whatever position they so exist in the Infinite Consciousness. When this principle is thoroughly understood, then the scientist can separate himself from his material world and place himself in an equitable position with other different transpositions of life as they are lived by mankind on other planetary systems.

Therefore the scientist will not seek ways and means to circumvent his seeming time-space dimension but will, in turn, do a more comprehensible thing; he will place himself in the terms of frequency relationship with other dimensions by the transference of consciousness wherein time and space are eliminated simply because he is now harmoniously, or compatibly, vibrating with whatever consciousness he wishes to attain. The old idea that there must always be a vehicle to transport consciousness is in-

deed fallacious and was born in the primitive aboriginal mind as it developed in the jungles and back
reaches of the world. Consciousness is not concerned
with any particular form of vehicle, for the transpo-
sitional element is strictly and basically that of a
compatible vibrating element. The vibrating element
can be considered to be so contained in such cyclic
patterns which, while being complete in themselves,
yet form the common aggregate of the Infinite Consciousness.

It must also be thoroughly understood in our
symposium or synthesis that there is nothing static
or apparently stationary in this Infinite Consciousness, but all forms and expressions as they are so
posed in the Infinite are continually, through frequency
relationship, regenerating themselves into new forms
of consciousness. Even the commonly associated
constituents of atomic forms as they are immediately
associated with your life upon the earth plane, are
undergoing such metamorphoses, internal changes
and structures; thus they are somewhat commonly
understood by present existing physical or atomic
scientists in these latter days.

Therefore, the reader must always remain conscious of the fact that he is immediately presenting
(so to speak), his face of consciousness toward the
Infinite. As he presents this face of consciousness—
with its five senses, in a physical sense—and relating
itself as it does also to its sixth or any number of
succeeding senses—which are merely more relationships as they are associated in energy wave forms
and are called extrasensory perception—this individual is also associating or relating himself to Infinity
and thus presenting his face in newer and different
aspects to the movement of the Infinite Cosmogony.

These are the common patterns of life as are posed
for every individual and which, in their basic deriva-

tions and extractions, thus place every human being upon an equitable plane with that of his neighbor. It does not, however, in any sense of the word, subtract from the individual's own personal position in his respect to the Infinite. As his position is always different from that of his neighbor in his understanding of the Infinite, he will therefore subtract such a position as he possesses and is able to interpolate in his consciousness into various extractions in his daily life.

This concept gives rise to the various racial differences and numerous other dispensations of life which are seen about you in your world. While these things are all a part of the consciousness of each individual as thus expressed and are vitally important to him, yet they mean absolutely nothing personal in the sense that they are so related to the Infinite Consciousness as a part of that continual resurgent pattern of regeneration in this Infinite Consciousness.

At this particular point, the reader will therefore be able to realize, in his present position and introspection to this Infinite, that the particular thing which was of the utmost and dominant importance is not the relationship of the Infinite to him but, his relationship to the Infinite. The Infinite is stable in all of its various and numerous manifestations and is considered a constant resurgent pattern of regeneration into all forms of consciousness, visible or invisible. Therefore, the reader will form in consciousness, various and conjunctive relationships with this Infinite which will or will not place him upon a constructive evolutionary pattern. This is the determinant of consciousness as it is posed by each individual in the more primitive misunderstandings of good and evil which will later develop into a much more harmonious, compatible understanding and relationship to the Infinite Consciousness. This then will become the

71

particular point of man's journey wherein he will have formed a stronger and more conjunctive relationship with the Superconsciousness, for the Superconsciousness is the Superego or the Christ Self, formed through numerous polarizations with the Father Within, as it is sometimes called, which is the sum and total of the Infinite.

Residing, as man has been previously supposed in our equations, in such nuclei or spiritual cell structures of frequency relationships with the Infinite Consciousness which, through this positive polarization process with the negative or the manifested earth life of any particular individual—he thus develops this Superconsciousness or Spiritual Ego to the point where it becomes the dominant polarity in his life. At this point the person will therefore exhibit and exemplify such interpolations of life which can be considered "Infinite" in nature and magical in their portent by any other individual who does not possess the necessary introspection to more properly evaluate what is commonly called supernormal phenomena, into natural manifestations of Infinite Consciousness. There is nothing supernormal in this Infinite Consciousness, but only becomes supernormal, magical or otherwise in its proportion, in direct ratio to how thoroughly it is misunderstood by the individual.

In the higher dimensions of life, supernormal phenomena is quite as natural in daily life as the materialistic, reactionary principles with which the materialist is presently concerned in his earth-life dimension. Consciousness of these facts in a subconscious way often gives rise to various and peculiar manifestations in the average materialist's life. As he has now reached a particular point in the evaluation of his own position with the Infinite, he has also entered into various other corrective syntheses in this position of his personal life and will thus become conscious to some degree—through the inner channels of consciousness of the manifestations of Infinite Consciousness about him.

Various other forms of life will begin to appear on the surface of the individual's consciousness which are exemplified into such forms as flying saucers and various psychisms which often relate him into flashbacks of past lifetimes. He will also begin to see or sense the existence of life as it is posed individually and collectively for mankind in the higher spiritual planes of consciousness. He will begin to conceive the possibility that life can and does exist in higher spiritual relationships where material dogmas, creeds and attitudes no longer make the individual subservient in a reactionary way to his daily life.

We can therefore never neglect in our own symposium, as we are concerned with the Infinite, that we should not at any particular point, delete from our present state of consciousness, by limiting our concept in our failure to understand the various and infinite number of subtractions as they appear upon the conscious surface of our minds, that this conscious surface is only one point of focus at the moment, where the individual is presenting his face of consciousness toward the Infinite.

The individual, therefore, who places his stamp of approval or disapproval upon any manifestation of consciousness upon the exterior surface of his life— or any other person's life for that matter—has only, in his ignorance, tried to place this same stamp upon the Infinite Consciousness. He has also tried to delete from the dismal and darkened regions of his own consciousness, the complete and Infinite Cosmogony, the very Creative Life Forces which gave him birth, the impetus to survive upon the planet earth and to propagate his existence into other forms of life in higher spiritual dimensions. Such ignorance is inconceivable and would exist only in the mind of an ignorant person. And yet such ignorance is found in comparatively high echelons of the scientific and other so-called higher factions of the material world.

CHAPTER 11

The scientist has until quite recently been prone to limit the span of life as it is found upon the earth to something which is relative and indigenous only to this planet despite the fact that through his telescope he sees a small fraction of this Infinite Cosmogony about him. Nuclear science, too, has propounded for the scientist, new equations in the term of Infinity, yet here again, he is prone to lay down the lines of demarcation and thus stamps himself with the same seal of abysmal ignorance as his contemporaries from the more material realms and dimensions of earth existence. In a true spiritual sense—and realizing the proportions of Infinity as so compounded in the extractions of the Superconsciousness and its conjunctive relationship with the Infinite—man becomes a man only when he realizes his own particular position in respect to this Infinite and when he has destroyed completely the illusion of self from his own particular position to this Infinite.

In this position of self and its false structure of the ego as it is compounded from Freudianism, man has used only the five reactionary senses which were compounded by him from out of past lifetime dispensations. He has not used the most valuable part of his existence and relationship to the Infinite as it is interconnected to him through other channels which are called extrasensory perceptions. Only in extrasensory perceptions can we find the true relationship to the Infinite, the true motivating libido or drive, the so-called "Guiding Light", the necessary virtues, the inspirational values which are so necessary to make the continuance of life through various planes of experience.

The individual who is vitally concerned with his own position in respect to the Infinite, will find many ways in which he can presently equate this position. Looking about him in his present world, he can find numerous ways in which various external manifestations are made in common union with thousands of others who are of like nature and who occupy a similar position. Such external dispensations which are found in political systems, religious orders, cultisms and in social structures, as well as in personal habits can all be considered to be extractions and developments along the pathway of life from previous lifetimes.

When such particular dispensations of life began to form a certain hard core nucleus, or when they can be strong enough in any particular person's life wherein they are worshiped or idolized, or form a dominant influence in that person's life to the partial or complete exclusion of all other things, then this person can be considered spiritually and somewhat mentally retarded upon his plane of life. He has temporarily, so far as the surface of consciousness is concerned, stopped in this evolutionary process.

Present-day examples of these past idolatries can be found in numerous dispensations about us. Such common extractions as were formed from previous pantheologies and understandings of so-called mystical forces and elements can be seen in the expression of religious systems and observances in the world about us. The common observances of Christmas, Easter or other religious demonstrations are in themselves, merely extractions and modifications of old paganisms wherein substitutions of deistic or guiding forces have been interwoven into the fabric of these expressionary counterparts. This fact is quite true of the individual who calls himself a Christian. There is actually nothing Christian in his attitude toward life, either in his day by day actions toward his fellow men or in the common elements wherein he continually judges and reacts according to reactionary values of force, dominance or the will to survive. He will therefore never be what he calls Christian until he can begin to express from the inner self, the true perspectives which are contained in the Infinite Consciousness.

The bended knee, the altar, the consecrated services are merely more recent forms of that age-old escape mechanism which has been the common subterfuge of man in all races and in all walks of life since the beginning of his evolution upon the planet earth. Whenever such particular psychic pressures were built up in the subconscious to a certain point, they were then most necessarily expurgated from the immediate consciousness—at least temporarily—by some particular witch doctor, who later developed into a priest in some specific religious dispensation. In this common escape mechanism, it can be considered that all the various political and religious systems are escape mechanisms, or merely a compromise wherein an individual seeks to escape his own moral responsibility and his position to the Infinite. He has not yet attained the particular position in life when he will shoulder his own moral responsibilities and realize the implications of past lifetime dispensations which were so materialistic and reactionary in nature.

In order to gain absolvency from these reactionary stances, he must adapt within himself and in his daily life, certain relationships which would relate him into higher spiritual planes of consciousness. He cannot do this by resorting to the common subterfuge contained in the daily confessional or the weekly rite (which he believes will purge himself of these various sins by attending some church), no more than can the so-called pagan or infidel accomplish the same results by ringing a temple bell or burning incense upon the altar. The two expressions here, whether paganistic or Christian, are basically and essentially the same. The old cliché of "the pot calling the kettle black", is applicable in this particular case.

Moreover, it is a common human weakness to continually exploit the pure essences as they were originally contained in such postulations of higher spiritual concepts, into weakened and watered-down versions which contain personal extractions and derivations from these originally pure essences. Altar worship has thus become a substitute (to some extent), for some of the more barbaric or paganistic rituals which often involved human sacrifices but the principles and ramifications involved, so far as they concern human evolution, are basically and essentially the same.

Man has not changed his perspective to the Infinite; he has only substituted for human sacrifice, his own particular identity and expression in his evolutionary flight into the Infinite; for in each successive subjugation to external deifications to such existing systems of idolatries as they are found in the world about us, only mean that the individual has made another one of the personal sacrifices which have been made from the very flesh of his own nature and the tears of recrimination which he will shed for himself in the future will be as the drops of blood from the former sacrifice.

Salvation is attained only when one assumes his own moral responsibility in his position toward the Infinite, his willingness to accept this moral responsibility in gradual attainment and an expansion of consciousness which will relate him to higher planes of relationship to this Infinite. There is no other way, for indeed any other way would be contrary to the Infinite Plan as it has been so conceived by this Infinite Consciousness.

CHAPTER 12

Now that we have discussed some of the more infinite abstractions of man's nature and the evolutionary flight of each individual through "time and space", let us examine some of the more materialistic or physical elements as they are concerned with present-day dispensations in the fields of such existing corrective therapies which are classified as psychology or psychiatry and medicine. In our present-day understanding of psychology, the practitioner or psychiatrist is devotedly Freudian and the principles underlying the Freudian psychology are quite well understood by both the practitioner and the student.

Basically, Freudianism is a reversion into the beginning of the Age of Reformation in Europe when a certain Scotsman named John Locke first postulated the empirical doctrine which is, substantially, that the human mind was a clean and polished surface at the time of birth, and as such, each individual, in the concourse of life being subjected to various psychic or physical experiences, formed and reformed different thought patterns in his daily conduct of life. Freudianism further completely sterilized previously existing concepts of psychology from various concepts which were termed instincts. Only one of these instincts has remained a basic and essential ingredient of present-day Freudianism: that extraction is the instinct of sex.

The practice of medicine as it is concerned with present-day dispensations is likewise in a comparatively primeval state of development, although technically speaking, there has been considerable information gained about the physical anatomy and its function in the past fifty years or so since the time of Pasteur; yet so far as medicine is concerned, no knowledge of the spiritual nature of man is included in these dispensations. Through statistics as they are currently existing, the fallaciousness, the incompleteness, the sterility of both psychology and medicine as it is now understood by present-day practitioners, should be obvious at this particular time. The high rate of incidence in our mental institutions and asylums is a clear indication there is much more to psychology than has been postulated in Freudianism.

The unanswered causes for various diseases in our civilized manner and way of life, too, is a mute portrayal of the abysmal ignorance of the true source and cause of disease in mankind, as it is so thoroughly misunderstood by our present-day medical practitioners. So far as psychology is concerned, the admission of even one instinct automatically destroys the whole fabric of such psychology, for if there were but one instinct, is it not conceivable there should be hundreds of other instincts which would support the otherwise unsupportable functions of our daily lives? The newborn infant who immediately begins to breathe, certainly could not have learned this breathing process from such intelligences as were commonly supposed to have been inherited through the gene structures or the chromosomatic cells in the process of insemination. Here again, is a direct conflict with all known scientific dispensations as they relate to the transmissions of energy wave forms in any particular forms of life, whether in the "solid" atomic particles or in radio transmissions.

Neither the psychologist nor the doctor has the slightest inkling of the more scientific and abstract principles behind life which we have previously discussed in these texts. Neither does the psychologist nor the doctor so combine any known or existing electronic, atomical or physical sciences as they relate to energy wave forms into his practice or therapies other than in the particular machine which might be called the encephalograph or the X-ray machine. But, in any case, the inclusion of these devices is not intended, in any sense of the word, to include the spiritual side of man's nature which is still hidden and unknown to these practitioners.

Let us consider scientifically for a moment just what the brain is and its relationship to human conduct in our present-day existence. The brain is composed of some twelve billion small cells; and while it is true that at birth this brain represents an organ which is still comparatively unfunctionable, it, like the intestines and many other parts of the anatomy, has not yet come into its full usage. However this does not, in any sense of the word, mean that in days to come in the life of this infant, such interpolations of consciousness in his daily life will form all of the functionable attributes of his brain.

Let us consider that each cell of this brain is likened to a radio tube, a vacuum tube or a transistor. In scientific parlance, we find in the case of the vacuum tube, there is a positively charged surface to a negatively charged electrode called the cathode. The emission of electrons or energy wave forms across this vacuum between the cathode and the plate, is further modulated by a third surface called the grid. In certain proportions of negative and positive equations, this grid modulates the constant successive or alternating pattern of wave forms as it stems from the plate and the cathode of the vacuum tube. In this oscillation of wave forms from positive to negative is contained the idiom of this modulation from the grid which passes on into succeeding stages of amplification or emerges in a convergence of sound as it is manipulated in a magnetic structure and a diaphragm in the speaker system.

Therefore, in all degrees, the brain can thus be considered in a pure sense—either as a cell or in a general conglomeration of cell structures—as merely a series of small transistors or vacuum tubes. The external consciousness is the modulating grid and, through the five senses, this grid structure in turn, modulates the constant oscillation from these various different cells in which these oscillations are basically and potentially supplied from the internal psychic structures of the individual. The positive or plate side of this oscillating process is the Superconsciousness; the negative or the cathode side is the subconscious or the past material dimensions through which the individual has passed.

In this oscillating process between this past subconsciousness and the positive Superconsciousness of the future, the present, in the grid form, constantly modulates this interchange or oscillating pattern of energy wave forms as it is passed between the two elements of this brain cell. More specifically, for instance, the various wave forms which are called light, in passing through the lens into the retina of the eye, are thus transposed into suitable frequencies and terminating on the ends of certain nerve structures in conjunction with each brain cell, then modulates this constant oscillating process between past consciousness and future positiveness as it is posed in the Infinite abstractions of the Superconscious Self.

A short time to digest the full importance of this concept will immediately present many ramifications which can be involved in this process we call life. In this oscillating process from the negative past consciousness to the positive Superconsciousness in the interplay of these cell structures called the brain, and in the proper terminology as they relate to dispensations of frequency relationships, various regenerative factors called harmonic structures—all as energy wave forms—can and do subsequently inflict, in many different ways, certain inharmonious relationships which, in turn, will reappear upon the surface of this individual's life in numerous different forms such as mental and physical aberrations.

Consequently, psychic shocks in the various forms of catastrophic happenings in the individual's consciousness can inflict tremendous malformations in the oscillating process in these various cell structures which are relayed through the medium of the hypothalamus (an organ of the brain), which acts as a medium or a cable of transference into the psychic structures. The rear portion of the brain is relegated to the more automatic functions of the body, such as the beating of the heart, peristalsis of the intestines, etc., while the frontal lobes of the brain are subsequently relegated to the more reactionary dispensations of life which are called reason. In all cases, however, whether we are subdividing the basic functions of these brain cell structures, the principle under which they function is basically the same. It only means we are terminating their point of consciousness into different portions of the inner psychic self.

In other words, the rear portion of the brain will, in turn, terminate so far as its automatic function in relationship to the body is concerned, in more primitive or past lifetimes with the individual when he was —through successive lifetimes—orienting himself physically into the way of life in this material world. The frontal lobe structures of the cerebrum, in turn, would terminate into psychic structures which were more basically concerned with the abstractions or derivatives from any particular reactionary elements which were presently superimposing themselves in his consciousness. This too, was a two-way process; while extractions were made on the basis of past derivations from experiences in previous lifetimes, yet there also was a definite correlationship as to the interpolations of such extractions and derivations into the immediate perspective in the way in which these things were commonly expressed to the outward world.

It can now be seen after some thought, the process of thinking would be quite impossible were it not so connected with the interior or the psychic self which supplies all known and unknown ingredients in the individual's life and which are not from such apparently terminated surfaces of the brain cells as they present themselves in modern psychology or in modern medicine; but that they are only the devices which we have similarized to the transistors or vacuum tubes in our modern electronic equipment.

In laboratories at this moment, scientists are developing certain kinds of electronic devices which, as cells, are able to retain a certain intelligence for an indefinite length of time. These cells when compounded with other functional attributes of vacuum tubes and associated circuitry, form what is commonly called a Univac or an electronic device which is capable of performing mathematical or mental feats which are beyond those of the human physical mind.

Therefore it is very easily seen, that to surcharge the surface electrodes of a device known as a capacitor or a condenser, that for an indefinite length of time—depending on the efficiency of the dielectric compound which separates these two surfaces—this surcharged surface can therefore retain its potential until it is discharged and re-manifests itself in the reverse fashion to that which it was first propagated on the surface of the electrode. This condition is the same which is concurrently existing in the brain cells, for the brain cells present, so far as consciousness is concerned, the surface of one electrode which is attached to the subconscious or the Superconscious part of the psychic self. This electrode will, in turn, discharge itself into the frontal surface of the conscious self when proper relationships of frequencies are met in the perspectives of the immediate environmental situation. This is an oscillating process; but more important to realize, is the fact that these brain cells in themselves contain, as basic elements of their makeup, certain characteristics which immediately relate them to definite and well defined spectra of energy wave forms as they manifest themselves from the subconscious to the Superconscious Self.

This process can be likened to the various stages of amplification as it is contained either in a radio receiver or an amplifying device, which is necessary to transpose the extremely high rate of oscillating wave forms, called radio frequencies, into demodulated audio-frequencies which are heard and determined by the human ear. This is one of the functions of the transistors or the audio-tubes for, in this process of detection or demodulation, the original component— as it was superimposed on a basic wave form as stemming or radiating from a radio broadcasting station—was retained but was transposed downward (so to speak), in frequency relationship, until it became compatible in its frequency expression to the vibrating surface of the human ear.

The same principle of this audio and radio-frequency device, which we call a radio, is applicable in the same scientific terminology to all known surfaces of the different cells of the brain; it also applies to many of the different nerve centers which are scattered in very strategic or advantageous points throughout the human system. These points, in turn, present to the psychic self a certain relationship on the basis of frequency and, in their interpolations of oscillations from the psychic body, will thus regenerate certain perspectives of interpretation into the physical world.

A sub-audible frequency of ten or fifteen cycles cannot be heard by the human ear but instead, immediately reacts upon such centers as are associated in the vicinity of the heart and known as the solar plexus. The vibrating surfaces of these nerve centers will, in turn, impart this transference of energy in this sub audible range, into various auditory nerve centers of the body and into the brain. The person in this temporary subjugation of an extraneous force with which he is not customarily associated, will, in turn, react and will feel ill.

The same process on the other end of the audiospectrum is also true. Frequencies of 20 or 30 thousand cycles per second are similarly superimposed into different bone structures of the head and, in particular, around the ear where, as cells, these structures of the bone act as sort of transducers which consequently stimulate nerve endings terminating on brain surfaces with which these cell surfaces of the brain are not customarily (in any sense of the word), used to associating. This disassociation will cause immediate distress to the person, even though he cannot hear the emanating source of this energy which is being superimposed into his brain structures.

CHAPTER 13

In this scientific portrayal of the principles and functions of the five senses and several of the unknown—and sometimes termed clairvoyant or supersensory perceptions—we have factually related man to an inner or a more spiritual plane of consciousness. We have proven conclusively that man does live as a spiritual or energy being just as he has always, from the beginning of his evolution and even into the beyond when his evolution started in certain conglomerations of sympathetic wave forms and formed regenerative nuclei or cell structures of spiritual energy. These, in turn, formed into aggregates of vortical patterns and thus started or propagated the evolution into that evolutionary pathway of time and space—and beyond the time of time and space—into the unknown where time and space became integrated factors of relationship and assumed regenerative proportions in the dispensations of consciousness, so far as they presented themselves to the Infinite.

We have now established a definite and scientific relationship of man in his existence with the inner self or the psychic body. We have also gained some idea as to the stratification of this inner or psychic self, as these various strata or plateaus can be likened in many ways to those which we shall find in the interdimensional concepts which we have previously discussed. In other words, the psychic self is a composite relationship of a large number of dimensions; each one harmoniously attuned to a supporting dimension in which it most properly functions. This in turn, is again reflected in the idiom of negative to positive transference into ever increasingly higher dimensions of conscious dispensations into the Superconsciousness and even beyond the Superconsciousness into the Infinite which is called the Father Within.

Life, therefore, has now assumed an entirely different proportion to that which is commonly associated with present-day dispensations of psychology or medicine. Any act of consciousness does and always will include an infinite number of ramifications as they are concerned in interdimensional relationships through frequency relationship functioning from the psychic self. No act of consciousness can ever be performed by any individual at any given time without its immediate connection to an infinite number of similar experiences which he has performed in past lifetimes. The number of steps which he takes in his daily life are immediately associated with his past life for many thousands of years, far back until he first began to develop legs and walk upon the surface of the earth as some primitive creature.

No, we are not trying to prove evolution as it is concerned in the Darwinian concepts but we are proving evolution as it is concerned with the spiritual metamorphosis of the cell structures and vortical patterns as they portray certain particular resurgent, re-creative and expressive values from the Infinite Consciousness. Man has always been too concerned with the immediate or the physical proportion of all things as they assume themselves in his five physical senses and his reactions to the immediate appearance of any objectivism in regard to the reactive function as it involved his five senses. This possibly presents at this time, one of the greatest of any existing paradoxes; that while all known dispensations of life and the function of life, all known concepts of psychology, medicine, religion and the various other elements and factors of life are always the result of the seemingly unknown and intangible which is called the Infinite, yet man knows little or nothing of this Infinite.

Perhaps it can be said that this is also the purpose of the Infinite Consciousness. In the essence of extractions from an infinite number of experiences as they thus polarize themselves in the abstractions of positive relationships to the Higher Self and ultimately to the Infinite, any individual can, in the future eons of time, thus develop into godlike proportions and express some of the more infinite propensities of this Infinite Consciousness.

The objectivism of past texts as we have presented them to you in this work, will now reveal the obvious abysmal ignorance in which man is presently revolving in this "timeless, spaceless void", and which is infinitely solid in all proportions. While this introspection will, in some way, tend to deflate some proportions of the conscious ego, yet it will in introspection—and if continued in the right direction for a sufficient length of time—relink any individual into a more constructive pattern of evolution in the future.

It must always be remembered that the immediate or the present is always the byproduct of the past in its sum and total of derivations and extractions, as present consciousness is largely supported from these extractions and derivations. However, there is always the other polarity which is part of that ancient and so-called Holy Trinity, the Superconsciousness which, subsequently, is constantly reflecting into itself these various dispensations of daily life; and in the derivations from past lives, making suitable extractions which, as it does, positively polarizes the idiom of these experiences to itself and thus develops the

90

individual's own personal Spiritual Ego.

Thus in the future eons of time, it is conceivable that this Superconsciousness will assume a much larger proportion of consciousness than it now does for any one individual so revolving in this terrestrial dimension. In that day and time when this Super-consciousness has assumed a large proportion of its reflective or guiding qualities into the daily life of the individual, he will then be increasingly stirred with the desire, the consciousness, the quickening of this Spiritual Consciousness which will begin to differen-tiate him and separate him from the material worlds of consciousness.

CHAPTER 14

Our present-day psychiatry is indeed crude and the practice of psychology as it is expounded in our various asylums and the so-called therapeutic treatment of the different aberrations is likewise crude; the only difference being that there is now some sort of humanitarian interest to the environment with which the mentally aberrated person is immediately concerned. In other words, the psychiatrist resorts only to a temporary change of environment hoping thereby to induce a permanent change in thought patterns. Such a procedure is extremely fallacious and will explain why it is that so little success is being concurrently displayed in our modern dispensations of psychiatric treatment.

To further expurgate any particular psychic misalignments, the psychiatrist often subjects more advanced aberrations to severe shock treatments. This therapy is indeed crude and primitive and immediately is reminiscent of many of the bygone practices from the pagan or more aboriginal days of the individual healing practices wherein holes were often scraped in the cranium to let loose evil spirits and other weird practices which subjected the individual to horrible and extreme torture. Blood-letting was a common practice in the Middle Ages to relieve various kinds of diseases in the body; and this too smacked of the letting out of evil spirits. The present-day psychologist, in subjecting the patient to a severe shock, can be likened somewhat to fixing a delicate watch with a hammer; the treatment is, as previously postulated, reminiscent of bygone practices.

Herein, too, enters another commonly misunderstood fraction of psychological dispensation; that is, the complete elimination of various obsessive factors which have entered into the person's life. Through frequency relationships in various negative dispensations, a person quite frequently not only links himself to past similar dispensations but, through frequency relationship, also links himself to an infinite number of similar negative relationships, some of which have no immediate personal relationship to him but which, through this frequency attunement, automatically at that particular moment, become just as much a part of him as anything else.

This includes a number of other ramifications involving energy wave forms which have been constructed by other different entities of human beings. Thus, this person in a negative dispensation, automatically links himself to these similar destructive configurations of wave forms as they were previously formed by some other entity. If that other entity is in a spiritual world, wandering about in abysmal ignorance, he is quite likely—through that frequency relationship—to associate himself immediately with the mental processes of the person who was originally instigating the negative expression into his life. This is an obsession. It can be either temporary or permanent; it can be thoroughly established, upon the precincts of frequency relationship, that such things do exist and are existing (to some degree), with every human being upon the face of the earth today.

In our everyday walk of life, we cannot associate ourselves with any immediate perspective of life about us without involving ourselves in that same frequency relationship which originally created that

93

particular dispensation, no more than we can attune a radio to a broadcasting station without the direct result of receiving the program then being broadcast. Obsessions in the form of entities, through frequency relationship can sometimes be permanent.

When such a condition is superimposed through this manner in the interpolation of life to some individual, he is usually considered to be mentally aberrated or insane, as the various concepts, ideologies and the other confluxes and configurations of energy wave forms from the obsessing entity are sometimes in direct opposition to the present external surfaces of the then existing interpolation of life of the individual. He will then do strange things and thus be considered insane and will be incarcerated in some institution. This concept is not to be misconstrued with any past existing practices of witchcraft as they are commonly expressed in the jungles and back reaches of the world—either in the present or in the past. Such present or past existing expressions are primitive in nature and lack the common essentials of understanding.

We can no more mix or mingle the differences of these past dispensations than we can mix or mingle our present technical knowledge in medicine of the human body with the past dispensations as they were posed by Galen at the turn of the Christian era. And while the old and presently existing forms of witchcraft do contain certain basic elements of truth, yet practices and expressions are crude and primitive and often unfactual, both in the way in which they are usually supposed to exist and the way in which their elimination is attempted.

In the future when such a person is thus diagnosed and is known to be obsessed by an entity which has linked itself through frequency relationship into the person's present expression of life, then the simple

94

and common procedure which is contained in the knowledge of this existing condition, will immediately present the necessary and suitable technique for the elimination of this connection. This is done first, by making the obsessing entity aware of what he is doing; secondly, by making the recipient or the one who is obsessed aware also of what is taking place. With the interjection of certain catalytic energies which are projected in a psychokinetical fashion in the process of this introspection, the frequency relationships between the obsessing entity and the person thus obsessed will be broken and changed so that the obsession no longer occurs. There is no hocus-pocus about this process; no beating of drums, no rattles, no jumping or dancing about or wearing of great masks; instead, just a simple presentation of known scientific facts and elements which are presently partially understood in our modern atomic sciences.

When our future sciences of psychology and medicine are merged and when they also combine in this union, the different concepts and other perspectives of consciousness which we have entered into in the relationship of the daily life of the individual, we can then empty our asylums, our prisons, our hospitals and turn these buildings into something else of a more useful purpose. Hospitals, asylums and prisons today remain only as monuments to the abysmal ignorance of mankind in his expression of the therapeutic sciences. They are but huge monuments of stone wherein are written in blood, the names of countless thousands of people who have gone down to early and needless death through the re-infliction of karmic substitutes and tortures into the nether worlds by this same ignorance.

This continual reversal into the primitive reactionary expression of life continues because it isn't understood. "It ain't so," are the famous last words of many a person and have condemned others, too, who were innocent, to early graves, needless torture and wandering about in the astral nether worlds until they could again reestablish themselves into a healthier pattern of evolution.

How much better it would be if these purveyors of science, these expressionists of the various therapeutic arts as they are so contained in our psychology and our medical science, could realize that their science, their expression was, in itself, an infinitesimally small portion of the whole of Infinity; if they could but realize this particular fact for just a few moments, they would then be prone to strike from their consciousness these famous last words, "It ain't so." These words always brand any individual who so utters them with the stamp of ignorance, an ignorance not only of his own purpose in life, but likewise his condemnation of all those with the same type of destructive ignorance with whom he comes in contact.

And so man is still continuing his mad reactionary pace into the future. The rumble and roar of his great machinery, as he builds and rebuilds his so-called civilized world, is but a continuance of past-age dispensations and refabrications of other temples, other fallacious concepts which perished because they were built upon the sands of ignorance. In laboratories, the rattle of the test tubes and other scientific impedimenta sounds more like the rattle of chains which bind a man to his terrestrial dimension. The wonderdrugs which he injects into his veins become an opiate for he will depend upon them and not the integrity of his own personal character for his salvation in the future.

To the cause of reason and to the White and Guiding Light of Wisdom, man will remain unbending and unyielding; but to his own particular conflicts in his daily life, he constantly bends his knee in humble subservience and yet from all this he must learn, for as a participle—a cell in the Infinite Consciousness, he is born again and again; and, through the seemingly never ending cyclic patterns of life and death, each man comes to the time and place when he meets his Creator face to face. In this meeting, he will join in a common union with sanity, with knowledge and with wisdom.

CHAPTER 15

It has been observed that it is much simpler to deny than to understand. This is quite true in respect to any particular person's individual point of evolution wherein he has not become conscious and cognizant of the various relative, inceptive dimensions of interpolations which have been discussed in previous texts. Most often a person so confronted with truths or concepts which are beyond his understanding, always resorts to the subterfuge of denial. More often too, it is found these people always resort to another common subterfuge which can be called finger pointing and by this simple device, which is a diversionary measure, they hope to detract not only their own personal attention away from their own inadequacies and weaknesses, but also hope to focus the attention of others away from themselves.

It should be understood that everyone, to a lesser or greater degree, supports a preponderance of psychic configurations from past lifetimes wherein he has incepted a large number of life experiences which have somehow been either sinful or unjustifiable in a higher expression of life. These various unjustified objectivisms, while they may not be manifest in a person's conscious mind, yet they always exert a certain pernicious effect into consciousness and the person is thus continuously subjected in his daily life to a vague sense of inferiority or maladjustment.

To compensate for what Freud called a loss or deflation of the ego, this person often will—whenever such particular psychisms reach more than normal proportions—set himself upon some sort of a pedestal, often attending various universities and medical schools wherein—in a submerged sense—the motivation primarily being that of attaining a certain position of power or supremacy over his fellow man; he will thus be able to reinflate the deflated ego which he has suffered from so many past life experiences. Freudianism in itself, while quite factual in some of the surface or elemental equivalents of the more reflex nature of the subconscious, yet is singularly devoid of any concepts which would relate man in his continuity either to the past or to the future. As a matter of fact, Freudianism itself was brought into being after Freud caught a chance remark from a professor who was teaching him in a Paris school, that when someone who was in trouble sought him out, the professor very angrily remarked, "Always trouble, there is always a woman at the bottom of it all, too."

Upon this irritated remark, Freud spent the remainder of his life developing a psychology which thus divested man of all his spiritual attributes and various connections with either the past lifetimes or the Higher Self. Because Freud did not understand the continuity of life as participating elements in frequency relationships, wave form structures, etc., in modern scientific parlance, he therefore set up a huge and preponderant edifice, coined from various superlatives—some of which were self-invented—and with the obvious intent and purpose that here again was a pedestal wherein he was attempting to justify and reinflate his own deflated sense of ignorance concerning the true knowledge of life.

Unfortunately, this false science has fallen upon eager ears and hundreds of thousands—yes, even millions—have directly or indirectly felt the influence of this evil ideology. It can also be said that by and large, the exponents of this false psychology in the various fields with which they are associated, either directly or indirectly, in controlling the various relationships and destinies of mankind upon the earth today are, in themselves, just as largely masochistic in the subconscious sense as was Freud. In other words, through past lifetimes, here again through the innuendo of sex as it was supported or purported by Freud, the same sense and preponderance of negative expressions in past lives which were mixed up with various sexual masochisms, were again consciously interjected into the present life through this obvious escape device.

Among the very first of the numerous interpolations and concepts regarding the true position of mankind to fall by the way when Freud took out his little hatchet and began hewing at the bastions of human knowledge, was the continuity of life expression as it found itself supported in what is commonly referred to as instinct. While it is acknowledged in common psychology that the various plant and animal life which inhabit the face of the earth today, maintain their expression of life strictly from instinct, yet man, save but one basic instinct, is much lower on the scale of evolution than any of this insect, animal or plant life, for he does not now have any other than one basic sexual instinct to support him in his way of life and all knowledge or wisdom must obviously come from the surface of the world about him.

The word instinct itself, is rather a seriously misunderstood terminology and a much better substitute would be the word intelligence. No one teaches the tiny spider how to spin a perfect geometrically designed web; no one teaches the duckling how to swim after it emerges from the shell. The scale of plant and animal evolution is filled from one species to another with outstanding examples and portrayals of the continuity of life as it is expressed in these various, countless thousands of species in their widely diversified patterns and expressions in this terrestrial planet. Whatever any particular species is doing to support its particular span of life, it is expressing a direct ratio or proportion of intelligence which was incurred from previous lifetimes lived in almost the identical manner and form to that in which it is presently occupying.

The fallaciousness of genetical science, too, is quite apparent when it is evaluated only on the surface as the transference of various characteristics as they are commonly supposed to exist in the genes and chromosomes at the moment of inception or conception. It must be understood that in our nuclear science it is common knowledge we cannot transmute one element into another without also altering all basic characteristics of the original element. Therefore, as genes are composed of atoms, how then—if they are to be transposed in terms of relationship from one lifetime to another—do they assume any proportions other than that which originally so compounded and supported them from the interior of their own dimension? The intelligence which a human or any other specie of mammalia, fauna or flora on the face of the earth possesses, is not supported from any genes or chromosomatic structures which originate in the process of insemination or fertilization.

Atoms are only adjutants to the expression of various continuities of wave forms as they are stemming into a certain sphere called life consciousness from a certain psychic cell or nucleus of life which is being expressed in an entirely different dimension from the material world. This is just as true with the new born babe as it is with the spider, or the duckling, or with any other particular species of plant or animal which you might care to examine upon the face of this earth.

The child coming into the world immediately begins an association of factors in his present environment which become compromised with derivatives or extractions of reactions from past lifetimes. This is strictly a problem of reorientation so far as the child is concerned, in an environment which is usually quite new and different to that which formerly supported him; that is, of course, except in such basic elements as the way in which he obtains his food, clothing and housing facilities which has remained basically and essentially much the same from one epoch of time to another. The configurations in which man lives, as they are portrayed in such examples of housing communities, structures, etc., have remained, to some degree, almost intact for many thousands of years.

While we may in this day have plumbing and electrical conveniences in our homes, it is also conceivable that many hundreds of thousands of years ago, the earth also supported civilizations which had a much higher and greater degree of freedom from the various physical expenditures of energy which were necessary in the more primitive stages of evolution. In other words, technocracy and automation were much more highly developed in the Atlantean, Lemurian or other cultures than exist in the present day.

Therefore, the newly born child immediately begins a whole system of reorientation into various factors of environment in which he finds himself from past life experiences. This will explain to the psychologist some of the otherwise unexplainable enigmas which relate to such factors as creative ability. The child who is considered a genius and begins composing music or expressing science to a high degree of relationship at the tender age of three or four years, is merely expressing a more realistic continuity of life from one lifetime to another than is customarily expressed by the masses and the multitudes who are in somewhat of a less favorable position to continue such expressionary forms.

However, the basic elements in the expression of life, whether they are more or less advanced, whether minor or major, these same principles remain inviolate and intact; whether they are necessary for the propagation of the amoeba from a one-celled animal into a similar amoeba through the simple process of fission into the not too distant future, or whether they have continued on up through any particular expression of life as it is found on the face of the globe. Yes, even into the atoms themselves, for atoms as they are synonymous in basic and elemental structure, one atom to another in its own particular orbit is portraying into the physical or material world a certain continuity of expression which is always supported from the interior surface of that atom's consciousness.

CHAPTER 16

In the practice of medicine, the doctor is also guilty of the same nefarious deviation from a true and constructive evaluation of life. While medical science has advanced considerably in the past fifty or hundred years, it yet remains for the future medical practitioner to bring out the true cause or origin of many of the diseases which are plaguing mankind today. It should be borne in mind by the reader at this time, that there is no particular quarrel with psychology or with medicine as it is commonly practiced today; for such psychology and medicine while in themselves are still primitive, yet they all combine to make up some sort of functional unit or step in the right direction. The main issue in all contexts or expressions wherein we have entered into discussions of this sort, is primarily against the dogmatic attitudes of the exponents of these sciences.

Along with the dogmatic attitudes which have been adopted by the exponents of these various sciences in setting themselves up on these false pedestals constructed from pure fabrication of truth, they have literally, either directly or indirectly, affected the lives and destinies of countless millions of people. They have incarcerated hundreds of thousands of souls into useless and needless years of pain and suffering; they have detracted them from their true evolutionary course. But even worse, with a far-reaching effect which concerns the average individual, there is the implication that every man does not possess a soul or that such concepts are not concurrently substantiated by modern psychological or medical practice.

The psychologist fails to properly understand an Oedipus complex—which is basically the sexual love of a male child for his female parent or vice versa —and therefore this complex will remain in rather mystical terminology not only in the minds of the psychologists but of anyone who so hears this particular expression. Therefore, from then on—so far as the immediate future is concerned—the complex which has been attributed to this child, remains an unsolved, mystical and undetermined element, simply because the psychologist fails to realize that in past lifetimes, the mother and son or the father and daughter were associated in various relationships as man and wife and built up between them in numerous past lifetimes, a very strong association of sex, which is presently reflecting into their lives in the usual manner and form, and in such vagaries and indispositions which the psychologist calls an Oedipus complex.

This same situation resolves itself into any one or a number or, as a matter of fact, into all different particular definitions of psychological parlance. Here again, the same facts are quite obvious in our modern medicine. While the scientists or the medical practitioners are quick to take any advantage possible to superimpose their supposedly abundant and prolific medical training, they are, to some degree, the delineators of life and death over hundreds of millions of people and seem to focus themselves in some sort of a sense of false security into the various supposedly virtuous attributes which they have incurred through their training. Yet, when the physician or the therapist is pinned down to the mat, so to speak, he will be reluctantly forced to admit that he does not know the true basic and originating cause of more than two or three hundred of the killers which are plaguing mankind. He will admit that only about twenty-five percent of the available knowledge of the human body is presently understood by the medical profession.

It is quite obvious that the other seventy-five percent of available knowledge is contained in diverse concepts which would relate man into the more spiritual dimensions wherein, if the physician could look into the psychic body and see through previous lifetimes and in affiliations and experiences, psychic shocks and numerous other interpolations of life in these past lives, he would find the true originating cause of the mental or physical aberration. A sword thrust which was incurred two or three hundred years ago in the breast of some particular person is very often found to be the seat of cancer in this present lifetime. A person can also suffer vicariously from seeing different catastrophic happenings which had taken place about him.

The supposed unknown cause of any disease and the knowledge which will subsequently lead to its elimination and cure, therefore, must always be found in previous lives. With the exception of a few comparatively primitive aboriginal tribes in the backwashes of the jungles of this world, by and large, most people have lived hundreds or even thousands of lifetimes and, as they have lived these lives idiomatically in any one particular time, place or civilization, they have incurred the various indispositions of these different lives.

The context of this evolutionary principle of life is contained in many different places in the literature of Unarius, as Truth will always bear repeating. Truth is a many faceted gem which needs constant turning to see the new facets, the new beauties and the new iridescence portrayed upon its surface.

To the exponent of our modern day classical psychology and medicine, may we say that almost every day the old forms of different concepts, as they were firmly believed and reoriented into life from these past dispensations are constantly being torn down. In the past fifty years we have seen the passing of many classical expressions of literature, science, philosophy and other different dispensations of life which came out of the various civilizations of the past.

Newton fell to Einstein, just as Aristotle fell to Galileo and so the pattern goes. Each day finds new concepts, new evaluations, new truths taking the place of those which formerly meant life and death to so many millions of people. On this basis it is quite safe to predict that, in the near future, our modern psychiatry, psychology and medicine will be just as primitive as that which we now consider primitive by looking back into the jungles and into the former witchcraft and pseudoisms which have existed in the past ages.

When that long-looked-for day arrives, then mankind will have found his Utopia, for in this common knowledge and in its daily expression, as he relates himself in a progressive evolutionary pathway which is linked into the future and into Infinity, mankind will gradually dispense with the reactionary practices with which he has decimated his world from time to time in the past ages. He will lay aside his warlike weapons, his cruel practices, his masochism, his various complexes which are founded basically in such primitive reactionary elements as would be found in the beasts which prowl the forests and the jungles of the nether regions. He will replace his hypocritical attitudes which have erected these pedestals for him and in their place will come strong and intelligent leadership which will light the pathway for succeeding generations of mankind to follow into a more proper relationship with the Infinite.

Just as he has done in the past, man will replace the asylums, the prisons and the hospitals with institutions of learning wherein mankind can gain a true and more comprehensive pattern of evolution. He will learn to cancel out the various physical and mental aberrations from the spiritual side of life before they have gained sufficient strength and intensity to cause physical and mental distress or even eventual death. He will learn that it is not necessary to remove an organ from the human body when it has become defective; instead, he will supplant this practice with a more realistic medical therapy of life which will relate to prevention and cancellation of a particular psychic shock or a vortical pattern of energy as it stems from the psychic self into the present consciousness. He will learn that such physical conditions as cerebral palsy, multiple sclerosis and various other present killers are, in themselves, a direct result of the evolutionary pattern of life wherein the individual has incurred certain misalignments through psychic shocks and other indispositions; and that reorienting the person into a true spiritual pathway, a true course of life, always removes the misalignment thus bringing about an eventual restoration of physical fitness.

It must be pointed out also, so far as the planet earth is concerned, that in the Infinite Universe in an astrophysical sense, the proponents of various astronomical or astrophysical sciences are just beginning to be vaguely conscious and aware of the great universe about them. With this awareness will come a new understanding: that in this interplanetary and interstellar dimensional space, as it is now called, will be found planetary systems and great worlds which far supersede our own physical world in all sense and proportion. The scientist will find man living in this Infinite Universe and in the many other Infinite universes which are surrounding this particular one.

Here again man will find himself living and expressing himself in an infinite number of ways, manners, forms and degrees of consciousness.

With this knowledge will come this obvious fact: the earth is comparatively low upon the scale of evolution so far as it concerns mankind, and on this planet, man has taken only the first step which will, in the concourse of time and many thousands of lives into the future, gradually separate him from the bestial propensities which engendered his existence into the material world. He will gradually learn that through this direct interpolation of oscillating wave forms with the higher forms of life and with the infinite propensities of the Creative Universe, that each individual is thus building for himself a certain dimension which is likewise Infinite in nature; thus man will, in that future time, become somewhat Infinite in nature.

By that time, man will have completely lost his physical form and, as a matter of fact, much of the common knowledge which he formerly used to support that physical body upon the planet earth will instead become knowledge and wisdom to support a new kind of life, a new body, and a new way in a dimension which could not possibly be conceived in his present-day consciousness. A cardinal principle in the personal development of any individual in this evolutionary flight into Infinity is contained in the precepts and in the concepts that each man is, in his own right and in his own way, his own personal interrogator, his own moderator and, in this sense, he also sometimes becomes his own judge, jury and executioner.

To those who would stray from the precept of this consciousness, may they be warned that to usurp the authority of dominion over their fellow man in any one or a multiple number of forms, as it is commonly associated in earth life dimensions, (whether you are king, emperor or simply an exponent of some of the medical or psychological professions in your time and place)—that this warning carries its own message; for if in some manner or form, should you be guilty of diverting another from the true course or purpose, should you usurp the authority or dominion of right which each person expresses as a direct prerogative from the Infinite Will and Consciousness, then indeed, you have incurred grave and sometimes disastrous consequences.

The false sense of security which the average individual learns to develop by focusing his attention into some of the medical or psychological practices of this day and time, could be an obvious and devious device wherein his true evolutionary pattern could at least be temporarily, if not permanently, misdirected and thwarted into one of the astral underworlds.

Thus, assuming proportions and a preponderance of an absolute moderator, in the sense that the physician or the therapist is in a position to alleviate all the ills of mankind, means that the medical and psychological practice is guilty of usurping the dominion of the Infinite Consciousness which is a direct adjutant of all people existing in any particular dimension. He is just as directly or indirectly guilty of this false assumption of power as is the king, the emperor or the dictator. This is also true of those who have set themselves up as demagogues in the educational profession.

Great universities are now flourishing throughout the civilized world and here the young men and women of the future are all put through holes of the same size and the same sieve and are figuratively given a parrot's beak when they receive their diplomas upon graduation, for now they must all speak the same tongue and the same language. They must all follow the same lines of demarcation, and woe be unto the person who dares to go beyond the limits or the boundaries which have been laid down so rigidly in these academic teachings.

This, too, is in direct contradiction to all known precepts which contain historical accounts wherein certain individuals in relating something basic or something good to the posterity of mankind, have always had to step out beyond the bounds of the recognized dogmas and creeds which were concurrently existing in their own dimension and time. These exponents have also suffered, either slightly or much; sometimes direct physical persecution and even death was incurred from the teaching, directing or the pointing out of truths to the race of mankind in a fashion or manner which was not dictated by the precepts of the various existing dogmatic and demagogic forces which were then in existence.

This was the fate of the humanitarian known as Jesus and history is filled with such portrayals wherein individuals have suffered in some manner or form, even to the point of death, for daring to go beyond the reaches of the minds of their fellow men in the systems which had been and were concurrently in force and motion.

During the Dark Ages in Medieval Europe in the time of the Reformation, it was estimated that more than three million people met their death at the rack, the wheel and the stake, all under the guise of being purged from the face of the earth as heretics, working against the name of Jesus the Christ. The list of names which could be extracted from those who have met martyrdom in this manner and form, would be one quite illustrious in nature and a very few indeed, such as Martin Luther and Galileo escaped this perditious practice of the Holy Roman Empire.

Our present-day civilization is not entirely immune

to the same practices; and while we do not burn people at the stake or tear them to pieces on the wheel or the rack, yet the demagogues of the professional world, as they express themselves either in religion, science, medicine or psychology, find their own way to destroy these brash individuals who have gone beyond the reaches of their own minds. They will not only be excommunicated from their own organized societies and the tenets of their own understanding, but such excommunications will also extend into various social structures. This is commonly referred to as "black-listing", and this modern expression can and often has, reached the point where the unfortunate exponent of a new truth has actually been railroaded into an asylum or into a prison.

Yes, he may find the faces of his loved ones, his fellow citizens, those with whom he formerly associated on a most compatible basis, will now turn away from him. He will find the very privileges of this society which were formerly extended to him, are now denied. Yet as it always has been, so it must always be; that as far as the earth and such similar dimensions of life are concerned, there must be those who are way-showers; those who must reach ahead into the infinite vistas and extract such suitable configurations of truth which will make life more compatible to succeeding generations developing along that dynamic principle of life expression.

Yes, it can even be said that those who in former lifetimes destroyed the exponents of far-reaching newer truths, often became in later lives their strongest exponents. Many of these people were responsible for the carved and graven images which were set up to those who so perished by their hand. Guilt in itself brings its own day of reckoning and, whether incurred in a previous lifetime and in the idiom portrayed from the nature of any particular individual—yet, in succeeding lifetimes as the individual progresses and presents a new face to Infinity and as the guilt or the wrongness of his actions eventually catches up with him, he then becomes his own judge and his own jury. Quite frequently, in the anxiety and the intensity of his guilt complex—as it is thus compounded from past infractions—he again assumes the false prerogatives which are contained in these pedestals which he has constructed for himself and which he will continue to erect in succeeding lifetimes, until he learns the true evolutionary path of life.

Sin is not a part of the Infinite Mind or Consciousness. Each man makes his own evil by wrongly using or by wrongly interpolating various constituents of life with which he is in contact at that moment. In future evolutions, these various past derelictions from truth now become the core or nucleus for a great guilt complex. It is so conceived in the Infinite Mind that each man shall learn of Infinity in his own way; for while in a complete and abstract sense, the Infinite can be considered perfect in all its relationships and expressions, yet mankind has found various and devious ways to circumvent the true advent and purpose of this Infinite Intelligence into his consciousness. It can be said, by this circumvention—by the continual and repetitious treadmill-like pattern of comparisons between good and evil that man manages to make derivations and extractions which will form a substantial platform into a future evolutionary pathway.

We have discussed the more fundamental concepts in the development of man's spiritual nature and in his relationship to the Infinite. We have also entered into discussions which will give man a much more realistic approach to the Infinite in which he will survive in these various spiritual transpositions. Also in our discussions, we have attempted to present a more equitable and basic understanding of the known and visible, or the third dimensional world wherein man lives at the present time and of his position to this third dimension or material world. All of these contexts would be quite meaningless in their entirety unless we could at least substitute a suitable and more expanded concept which would completely explain and justify all of these known precincts within the realm of our third dimensional science. In this discussion we shall thus enter into and present to the reader a much more realistic approach, not only to our third dimensional science as it is concerned in the world today, but also to enable him to integrate this science into an expanded consciousness which will involve the Infinite Cosmogony.

CHAPTER 17

In the realm of physical science today, we are seeing a great change or metamorphosis which can be called the beginning of the "space age", wherein man is attempting through rockets and in different ways, to shoot satellites into orbit around the earth. He is also attempting to shoot rockets to other nearby planets, the moon and also the sun, with the possibility of establishing relay systems and other types of devices intended for communication purposes so that he will be able to form somewhat of a more comprehensive idea of the entire universe. This is indeed, from a more advanced position, rather a silly procedure, inasmuch as Infinity is in his immediate environment. He has only to stretch forth his hand and touch Infinity in all its different directions and in all its ramifications.

By substituting his mind for his hand, he could thus bring into realization all of these various implications into his present-day science. In this day and age, too, it does present many strange paradoxes in the realm of physical science and starts with the most advanced of these scientists in the days of the Reformation. It was Newton who established many different physical laws and mathematical formulae which were very valuable in the succeeding hundreds of years in helping to establish a physical science upon the face of the earth.

It was Einstein who, to some degree, disproved much of the Newtonian concept, except possibly that wherein Einstein approached the concept of light, both he and Newton made the same common mistake as that made by all other scientists, including those in our time: they were trying to equate the whole Infinite Cosmogony on the basis of a few reactionary manifestations in their physical world. The most classical example of all of these singular paradoxes exists in the realm and concept of light. Today science is concerned with the transference of light from any given point at the predetermined rate of 186,210 miles per second. This speed of light apparently represents, at the present time, the last known barrier between man and the infinite reaches of space.

We have in the past, just as today, witnessed the falling of many time-hallowed concepts in our physical science which have arisen from various scientific dispensations. For instance, the so-called sound barrier disappeared some years ago; and at the present time, our United States Government is building superbombers which will travel through the stratosphere at a speed of more than twice that of sound. At the present time, the explorations into space are limited by another seemingly insurmountable barrier which is called the thermal barrier; or in other words, trying to achieve escape velocities from the gravitational field of earth without burning up the vehicle through friction of the various molecules of atmosphere against the skin surfaces of the airborne vehicle.

In the near future, the thermal barrier will also disappear just as the sound barrier and this will leave possibly one remaining barrier—the speed of light—to man's escape into the more proper understanding of the Infinite. Science, through a common and basic understanding, has related the various transpositions of energy as they are concerned in different spectra of light, radio waves and other such emanations, into the extreme and predetermined rate of 186,210 miles per

116

second. This too will vanish in the more distant future, simply because there is, in the world of science today, an understanding of speed which means we have equated the appearance of one particular objective form of energy from one point to another at a predetermined rate of speed. It has not occurred to the scientist that so far as the physical or the third dimension is concerned, all the various manifestations of energy forms as they are concerned with the more immediate fourth, fifth and sixth dimensions which are in close proximity to that of the earth, and all these different appearances or manifestations which he calls the speed of light, are only transferences of energy from one dimension to another.

Close to the turn of the twentieth century, Max Planck was walking quite close to the line of truth in this respect in his "theory of quanta", which Einstein later picked up and, through various mathematical equivalents, was able to continue on into what he called the "space-time continuum". He almost factually proved that the existence of the common barrier of light of 186,210 miles per second was fictional so far as the fourth or fifth dimensions were concerned; and that in free space, light had an undetermined rate of speed and could not be calculated except when other, somewhat unknown factors, were entered into which related to any particular given amount of light in its position to the infinite space.

We can gain a more comprehensive idea not only of space-time continuum but into the physical world about us when we realize this third dimension in which we are presently living, can be considered parasitic in nature. That is to say, whether we are concerned with any constituents known as the 100 atomic forms of energy or any other particular known physical laws, these things are in themselves, only relationships of energy as they are transformed from one dimension into our immediate perspective which is done on the common basic equivalent of reactance or resistance.

Any present-day known physical law which is taught in high school can be reduced to this simple analogy: we are merely presenting in our third dimension—so far as it is concerned in our immediate perspective, the movement of energy which becomes reactive to any one or a number of other forces which are in existence at that particular moment. The centripetal, centrifugal, inertia and various other so-called laws will thus be seen to be reactive constituents in this concept and energy, moving as it does in a dynamic form, is constantly in conflict with numerous other different static forms of energy in this third dimension.

Let us consider for a moment a more realistic approach to compounding within our own consciousness a much more suitable equivalent than that of the known light barrier (of 186,210 miles), to something which will give us a broader and more expanded consciousness of the Infinite Cosmogony. It has been definitely proven in countless ways, that man does exist in other dimensions, or in various other states of consciousness wherein he is not connected to any physical body. These provable manifestations have been called spiritual in nature and should be quite obvious to the classical scientist who has continually —at least up until the present time—completely ignored these various interpolations of spiritual life about him, inasmuch as he always termed them "pseudo" simply because he could not relate them into such common denominators of his physical science. This same problem which is extremely foolish in all respects, is being carried into interstellar or interspace activities to a high degree.

The speed of light could therefore be much more

easily determined if the scientist would learn to equate the speed of light or various other energy wave forms, as they appear in a reactive sense in his physical world, as merely the transference of any given quanta of energy from the infinite so-called "void" about him, into a form of energy that he could reactively equate in his own third dimensional hypothesis.

We must remember in our equations that the earth, just as the sun or any other of the heavenly bodies —whether it is concerned with our own immediate planetary system or represents a galaxy or part of a universe in the far-off and seemingly distant space— represents only certain focal points of energy transferences from other dimensions into the immediate perspective of the visual eye, so far as they are concerned in reactive elements or constituents of our physical science. If the scientists would consider for one moment the fact that space is infinitely solid and filled at all times and that the earth, like the sun and various other planets, is merely a tiny atom—or a point of focus—wherein energy is stemming into this third dimension in numerous ways. One of these ways is through the various forms of atoms which he has found in the world about him; another of these ways is in the transference of heat, light and numerous other reactive elements into the electromagnetic fields of force around the various atomic constituents.

The earth, the sun and various other planets or such visual points of focus can therefore be called terminating points in a relationship which can be similarized in a positive and negative equation. In all of these transpositions of energy, as they are concerned from positive to negative in the various electromagnetic spectra or fields which surround these numerous planets—as they do in every atomic form—we are here again merely "tapping" the Infinite Energy from the cosmic universe about us.

Therefore so far as the earth is concerned, the sun represents a somewhat more positive polarity inasmuch as there are various spectra or transferences of energy from a great vortical pattern supporting the sun; thus the sun does represent a more positive or catalyzing and polarizing field of force into the immediate electromagnetic field of the earth. If some giant hand momentarily dropped a great shield upon the surface of the sun and thus shut off all different energy transferences from the sun to the earth, we could not imagine for one moment that these energies were traveling from the sun to the earth in six minutes time, and that the terminal of these energy velocities—as they had started from the sun to the earth—would continue to travel to the earth without their EMF or the force behind them.

Therefore, when the giant hand dropped its curtain down over the face of the sun, the immediate terminating point of these velocities of energies would cease instantaneously—not in the six minute period which would be incurred if the scientist were correct in his hypothesis that light travels from one given point to another. Likewise, if this same curtain was jerked from the surface of the sun, a resumption of energy transference would immediately occur between the sun and the earth on an instantaneous basis, and not in the matter of minutes as it is believed by the scientist; simply because the sun would then immediately resume its normal function as a polarizing agent in the transference of energy from another dimension into our own immediate perspective or horizon of transference. Or, in more scientific parlance, this would again be established in that oscillating condition between the positive Infinite Cosmos and our own negative material world.

We must repeat and reestablish these concepts within our minds so that in this intercosmic under-

120

standing, we can completely eliminate such concepts as the transferences of energy as they are known in the scientific world—as heat, light, sound, etc., especially so far as light and other types of radioactive phenomena are concerned. As these lie in a more immediate and closer relationship to the Infinite, their speed of transference is much greater from one point to another.

However, this is not to be confused with the speed of light, or the terminating velocity of our known physical sciences, for the scientist has only equated this terminating velocity, as he terms the speed of light, to such closely allied radio frequencies which lie in the immediate spectra of light and such as are broadcast from our radio broadcasting stations. These energy wave forms—in all common sense and proportion— also vibrate or oscillate in the borderline condition of energy transferences from the third into the fourth or cosmic dimension.

Light in a pure sense, means only that we have transferred the relationship of certain energy wave forms into their vibrating frequency from the retina of our eye into the tiny little transistors called brain cells which, in turn, step up these energies into suitable wave forms wherein they can oscillate into the centers of the psychic body and thus relate to us, consciousness and form as it was incurred in previous dispensations of time.

The same principle is carried on into the cosmic universe about us and we are again manifesting consciousness through different agencies known as electromagnetic fields; and the appearances of various energy wave forms are byproducts of different forms of cosmic hysteresis in our present-day physical world. In the future, the scientist will be much more concerned with the different appearances and manifestations of life in other dimensions than those with which he is so presently concerned. When he has thus arrived at this point in introspection with the Infinite Cosmos about him, he will then not need to create some sort of a vehicle to transport his frame of flesh from one given point in this infinite universe to another; but he will be able, through suitable and various types of oscillating mechanisms, to actually change the basic oscillating frequency of the various atoms in his body as well as in other different atomic forms about him.

Thus, if he so wishes and adheres to the physical body to the degree that he believes it is necessary to transport that physical body in some given form, from one point of the universe to another, he can do so in an entirely different dimension than that of his now existing material consciousness. This was done 2000 years ago by the Avatar who walked upon the surface of the water of the sea of Galilee in the Holy Land, and walked through walls and did other types of seemingly magical phenomena which are called "pseudo" by the present-day scientist.

Other outstanding examples of this frequency transference in the relationship of atomic forms to the Infinite Cosmos has been exemplified in other parts of the world. We can still see, to some degree, some of these present forms of previously existing manifestations in our own present-day world, such as various forms of fire-walking; or we could search the back reaches of such empires as India and find super-normal phenomena, which could only be explained in common terminating points which involve inter-cosmic understanding.

This all means that in the future, if the scientist continues to adhere to his present-day hide-bound attitudes of classical science, he will make little or no progress; and all progress of science at the present time has been done in that stumbling, blundering and idiotic fashion wherein he has succeeded through constant and sometimes abortive attempts to thwart some seemingly known physical laws and finally arrive at some interpolation of concept in his own mind wherein he has proven that the known barriers of his physical science were actually nonexistent.

For the moment then, it is possible to consider that in the future man will understand, as far as the mind is concerned, the way in which it might consciously integrate itself with the Infinite Cosmos; that the mind could and would, as a necessary means of combining various concepts within itself, simultaneously relate any one particular individual to one or a hundred different points of junction. In this sense of the word, too, man could be considered in the appearance of realization as consciousness in his own immediate mind, that he could thus be actually existing in any given point of the universe or in any given number of points of the universe simultaneously.

CHAPTER 18

Concept is only one of these adjutants to understanding and, in understanding or realizing it in its full intensity, so far as the individual is concerned, man has actually eliminated all known barriers of time and space in his own immediate reactive physical world. The body, as a vehicle wherein the twelve or fifteen million brain cells have thus been impounded, means little, or is of absolutely no consequence whatsoever in regard to the fact that we are immediately concerned with objectifying consciousness in any part of the Infinite Cosmos. When this is done through a system of relationships and through existing forms of energy transferences known as vibrations, oscillations, or cyclic patterns of interdimensional relationships, it merely means we have linked ourselves infinitely to this Infinite Cosmos with any one or a number of given points of perspective.

When this particular symposium is carried into a little higher dimension of relationship—as man is a product of evolutionary circumstance—he will, in developing this particular relationship of life to himself in the future, also build the seemingly necessary energy body wherein he will be able to express, through various centers of this energy body, the necessary polarizing and catalyzing forms of energy which will actually integrate him with this Infinite Cosmos. This will explain to the religionist, the theosophist, or the cultist, the actual existence of the human embodiment in some higher or spiritual dimension.

This is not done through the living form of flesh in future days of the resurrection, as it is expressed in our modern-day Christianity, wherein the Christian believes that somehow his body will be gathered together when a certain horn-blowing takes place. Actually, he will be able in some period of time—such as a millennium—to integrate sufficient wisdom into his mind so that he will see the possibilities of living in another world which is not material in nature; and that his body will be composed of pure energy wave forms in different polarity patterns which can be similarized to the various organs of his body in their functional relationships to him and to the Infinite Cosmos.

In that far off and seemingly distant future, as far as the materialist is concerned at the moment, he will no doubt possess the necessary understanding so that he can look into this energy body and see its functional relationship to the Infinite Cosmos about him, just as he can see and relate his own physical body into his own immediate physical environment. The various organs of the body, as they function in a physical sense, are quite well-known to almost everyone in this day and age and the various ways and means in which organic chemistry is sustained in this body is also, to some degree, known to everyone. In the future thousands of years when people have developed consciousness to the degree that they can see themselves living in this pulsating energy body and that the various centers in this psychic or spiritual body are just as realistically integrated as are the various poles in the more Infinite Cosmogony about them, they will then indeed be spiritual creatures and will no longer need to return to the earth.

This is one more of the infinite ways in which the great Universal Mind, or the Originating Creator of all things is thus concerned by maintaining Infinity into all finite abstractions of various interdimensional relationships. This Universal Mind is infinite in all things, and in so being infinite, must therefore maintain this finite abstraction into all things.

Man, as he is posed and lives and equates his physical world is and will be just as he has always been, only one of the infinite number of points of introspection which any individual will maintain for any given point of time in his travels into the Infinite. This material dimension is actually the beginning of the evolutionary process which will carry him into the higher spiritual worlds where he will live in the future. He is in this way, in expressing his material world, only polarizing the various forms of consciousness as they are contained in the more complete abstractions of the higher Superconsciousness, as it has been posed and explained in previous contexts.

Quite necessarily then, the various adjutants which would support this consciousness in a suitable physical or material environment, have also become part of this environmental transposition wherein he can live and manifest life in different and suitable agencies for its expression. In part then, man's abysmal ignorance can be somewhat justified on the basis that he is still comparatively a very primitive creature, in the eye of this Infinite Consciousness. His greatest and most difficult problem as to the immediate present is to free his mentality and his concept of the world about him from the more immediate reactionary plane of existence wherein he has, through his physical science, attempted to justify the Infinite Cosmos and thus to free himself from his binding pit of clay. He can develop consciousness to a degree which will more suitably integrate him with Infinity and in relationships which are much higher and much more spiritual in nature.

Man can therefore be considered in true essence,

a creature which is still not completely man but is actually very strongly related to the animal kingdom upon which he depends for his very existence. Man, in his daily life, is still exhibiting many of the more animal-like characteristics and attributes from which he sprang, such as giving birth to living young and suckling them upon the breast, just as do the animals in the lower kingdoms about him. He is also quite as guilty as some animals in various expressions of passion, such as hate, avarice and the will to survive which gives him the necessary destructive intents wherein he will actually destroy his fellow man to support that in which he believes, in the various ideologies for his own existence.

If he could only realize before he fired a gun or exploded an atom bomb, that the Infinite Cosmogony is quite capable of supporting not only all of the known inhabitants on the face of the earth in a much higher state of consciousness but that there are also an infinite number of human beings living in various dimensions all about him and also in much different states of consciousness. Should he at any time, before firing these weapons of war, obtain within his own inner consciousness some glimpse of this Infinity about him, he would quite likely throw away these weapons and warlike attitudes and start to live for the day wherein he would more fully justify in his own consciousness, one of these higher forms of life.

Unfortunately however, as far as time is concerned —and as time is the necessary adjutant in these material worlds for the sole and express purpose of relating any individual into a natural sequence of consequences—the average human being, as he exists on the face of the earth today, is quite necessarily living in the age and time which he has justified by previous lifetimes. In other words, as a product of evolution, through hundreds or thousands of lifetimes, man has built himself up to his present state of consciousness and is fully expressing it in the material worlds at this moment. We are therefore not concerned with these materialists who believe so strongly in complete justification of all known material values in their everyday life; but we are more immediately concerned with those who have gone beyond this point into some of the more spiritual abstractions in which they have, either consciously or intuitively, incepted into consciousness various experiences in past lifetimes as well as such interpolations of consciousness in which they have lived in spiritual worlds in the lives between earth lives.

Every person does, from the time of death until the time of rebirth, live in some spiritual world, and to the materialist this is indeed a very nebulous, gray and hazy world wherein he finds himself without his physical body, simply because he does not have the necessary forms of consciousness to maintain a conscious relationship with the spiritual world in which he finds himself; and all of his values of life are posed upon material values which no longer exist in the spiritual world about him. Consciousness to this degree, however, is fortunately not completely justified in all intents and purposes, for overshadowing any human being in this nether world of spiritual values is that Higher Superconsciousness, that spiritual cell or nucleus, which has been created in cyclic patterns by the Infinite Consciousness.

These guiding and motivating forces which are constantly stemming into the psychic body of the person who is wandering about in the spiritual nether worlds—without form or substance—sometimes do, and will eventually in some succeeding spiritual world, (in the life between lives), lead him into such plateaus of understanding wherein he can see his fellow men about him existing in different states of spiritual consciousness. He then begins to form within his own mind the will and the desire to elevate himself into a more realistic position with this Infinite Cosmogony. Therefore, in succeeding lives on the earth plane, he will consequently seek about him in his present physical environment the various and necessary forms of life wherein he can justify what he intuitively or inwardly knows to be a higher form of life. Thus he has been spiritually quickened to a degree wherein he now wishes to shed the material world in all its entirety and in all its implications. He will also be quite conscious and keenly aware of all the various deficiencies in the material world about him. He will become much more alert and aware of the intense suffering going on in the various hospital wards, asylums and prisons in this physical world. As a consequence, he will be imbued with a greater desire to help relieve these sufferings, for somehow within the reaches of his inner self is oscillating a former pattern of relationship lived in a spiritual world and in a higher plateau of understanding.

To this person, therefore, can be given the message of hope; should he continue on in his pursuance of a higher Spiritual Way of Life, he will eventually escape the domain and the dominion of this physical world and will gradually evolve into one of these higher worlds of consciousness.

We, therefore, who have been spiritually quickened and are aware, cannot be deterred from our purpose of evolution into these higher worlds; nor will we be intimidated by the various coercive agencies which are expressed about us in the world today. We will not be driven from our forward path of evolution by snide remarks that we are "queer people" or we have "queer ideas", neither shall we take the various compounds of philosophies as they are extracted from this physical world and physical science about us, as the ultimate values in this spiritual evolution. We also thoroughly understand that these values are just as necessary to the materialistic minds as our spiritual values are necessary to we who have been so spiritually quickened; that they too, are undergoing that common metamorphosis—just as we did in the past —and in the future, their guiding Light of higher Spiritual Consciousness will eventually lead them into a higher relationship of spiritual values and will point out to them—quite obviously—not only the necessity but the complete feasibility of life in the higher worlds without the necessity of the physical existence.

Therefore, life in these spiritual worlds is not a mystical supposition—as it is posed in various pantheologies, cultisms and even in our modern Christianity—but is a factual and realistic development of life. It means an integration of heretofore unknown elements of interdimensional transpositions into everyone's daily life and, as the Infinite is filled with an infinite number of different interpolations of life, through consciousness, we automatically select such environments and such inclusions into our lives as make these things compatible with us. We also develop the necessary vehicle of transposition, such as the various bodily forms and the other environmental factors which help to polarize and justify the life which we find in these higher spiritual dimensions and make life much more compatible and suitable to us, even more so than we shall find in our physical dimension at the present time.

For indeed it is so, that when we have realized this spiritual life has been completely freed from the sins and iniquities, the dogmatic patterns of interpolations of the physical plane, then it must also be that we shall live in complete freedom from them, for they shall no longer exist in our consciousness. Instead, we shall supplant these patterns with a more infinite interpolation of life wherein we shall begin to oscillate, through common centers of intelligence in our spiritually formed body and mind, into the various infinite reaches of the Cosmic Universe. In that day and time—if it can be called time—we will have justified our search for Utopia; we shall have found our New City of Jerusalem, as it is called by Christianity; we shall have found that Nirvana, as it was termed by Buddha; the Happy Hunting Ground by the American Indian; and we shall have found any one or any particular type of Heaven which has been vaguely visualized by the inhabitants of the earth in one period of time or another.

Man must not create for himself an escape mechanism simply to escape the earth, without forming suitable relationships with the Infinite into which he shall travel in the future, for if he does seek to escape the world simply because of its worldly implications without suitable knowledge of the future, it would truly be disastrous to his forward path of evolution and would only incur greater amounts of suffering and so-called karma in future lifetimes and dispensations. Therefore, it is wise and it is well that we be constantly alerted in our future way of life, to impound as much of the higher spiritual values of life as possible; to completely do away with and tear down, the known limited barriers of physical consciousness and to realize that the Infinite Cosmogony—as it is within—can be realized within the precincts of our own immediate consciousness, for this is indeed the only true way of all men and the purpose of all men.

"Gather ye not treasures of earth for rust and moth to corrupt but rather, gather ye treasures in Heaven."

CHAPTER 19

No work of this kind could be considered complete without including the much talked of present-day physical phenomenon called cosmic rays, for in the precincts of various concepts which involve cosmic rays, their origin and manifestation, will be found several of the most important equivalents in the Infinite Creative Cosmogony. At the present time, science knows considerably more about cosmic rays than it did at the beginning of their discovery but it is commonly admitted by scientists alike, that their source or origin is still unknown. Present scientific terminology classifies many types of cosmic rays and, while these are primarily of interest in an academic sense to the scientist alone, we shall therefore not discuss them categorically or in such lengthy presentations, as further study along these lines can be pursued by the student who wishes to do so, from such concurrently publicized concepts existing at the present time.

Briefly, cosmic rays relate to a certain type of small electronic energy particles which are entering into the earth's atmosphere at tremendous rates of speed and these small electric constituents—to the scientist—represent a solid bit of matter. Yet here again, the scientist is confused by the terminology of what is called solid and he will find, in the future dispensations of science, that this seemingly solid particle will again resolve itself, whether it is an electron in an atom or a cosmic ray particle and it can be determined in this resolution, to again present sub-infinity in another sub-atomic or sub-electronic form and he will be impressed by the common symposium or comparison to our present solar system.

The actual discovery, as far as modern science is concerned with cosmic rays, started almost one hundred years ago, in the late 1800's, from a commonly devised laboratory device called an electroscope which was simply a small glass sphere or globe wherein, upon a short glass pedestal were fastened two one-inch squares of thin gold leaf. It was found when subjecting this sphere to an intense radiated field of magnetic energy, the trapped air within the sphere became ionized or charged; that is, each molecule of air assumed a certain charge of electricity and, under normal conditions when the stimulating or the magnetic field was removed, this ionization would disappear. However, this ionization was found to immediately cause these two small pieces of gold leaf to fly apart at right angles and to remain at this obtuse angle over a long period of time wherein, by simply removing the electromagnetic field of force, they would have normally collapsed into their normal position. This slow rate of discharge in ionization was found to be supplemented by an external field of radiation, which has concurrently developed into our existing knowledge of cosmic rays.

It was first presupposed that this external radiation came from close association with the earth itself. However, in the early 1900's, experiments made by climbing mountains and balloon ascensions determined that the rate of precipitation of this electronic field was increased as altitude above the earth's surface was increased. In other words, the atmosphere formed some sort of a point of absorption, so far as this cosmic radiation was concerned. With the invention of the aquarium-like device known as a cloud chamber wherein a quantity of fog-like gas was imprisoned, cosmic rays could be seen to make vapor trails across this fog-like gas and thus be photographed. While the particles themselves have never been photographed, yet the scientist possesses thousands of photographs of various types of vapor trails left by differently charged kinds of cosmic ray particles.

At the present time, science has subdivided into various categories and divisions, about 20 or so different types of cosmic ray particles and he has determined, according to such positive or negative or combinations of electronic charges contained therein, their life duration, speed and the amount of curvature which they attain—either to the right or to the left—when entering into the earth's magnetic field.

However, science does not yet know the exact source or origin of these cosmic ray particles. With this thought in mind we shall enter into a new field of introspection which will open up to the reader a new vista or a new horizon of creative thinking wherein he can actually see within his mind's eye, just how it is that the seemingly so-called particle masses as they are presented by the earth, the planets, the sun and various other stars in our galaxy or our universe or even universes beyond were created—and even the very sustaining processes of the atoms themselves. For in a common term of reference, so far as the different kinds of energy transferences are concerned, they are synonymous in nature and relate in all respects, however, into such fields or dimensions which are presently unknown to our modern scientist. Herein is a case where the old adage is used, that the "tail is wagging the dog" for the scientist has been attempting in these different directions of investigation and research, to determine and to equate the whole Infinite Cosmogony on the basis of the few interacting developments in his third dimensional perspective.

At the present time, science believes cosmic rays to be originating from some distant part of our galaxy, or any given point in the outer dimensions of interstellar space from such various refractories as are contained in the expurgation of certain particles of energy into "free space" from suns or other types of heavenly bodies, exploding stars or nova. It is believed by the scientist, in going through this so-called "free space", these tiny electronic particles begin to be batted about in a ping-pong like fashion from one particular sun or its electromagnetic field to another, and thus they start to attain these incredible velocities. It is known at the present time that various cosmic ray particles can penetrate as much as twelve feet of lead or go to the bottom of an ocean two miles in depth. They can also penetrate, at an incredible speed approaching that of light, through the very heart or nucleus of the atom itself, which is different than any other kind of energy our present-day scientist has as yet succeeded in generating.

If this ping-pong effect is true, then here too, we would find that science would defeat itself in its purpose of trying to relate a true and factual reason for the existence of matter in his present terrestrial dimension. In common everyday physics, nothing can exist without a cause and the basic cause of matter itself is whether it is concerned with the radiant field of force around the sun or into such other particular types or junctions of introspection. The scientist has not as yet, in this supposition of the Infinite Cosmogony, established anything which is relative to the actual existence or the procreative factors of existence in his material world.

Therefore we must start at an entirely new point of junction in our introspection which is far removed from our present known physical world as it is presented by the earth and the various star clusters around us in the Heavens; for all stars, solar systems, galaxies and universes can be considered only as tiny bits of surface matter which are floating upon the mind of the individual's consciousness.

It was told in some of the preceding pages that space was infinitely solid and presented, so far as reactance or resistance was concerned in different dimensions or in different spectra, a relative or quantitative amount of dimensional forms of energy, as they are posed in atomic structures in our present-day physical science; and conversely, so far as the Infinite was concerned, we could also have an infinite number of other existing energy forms which were not known in present-day forms of reactance or resistance to any of our five senses.

Now we shall find out just how it is that this seemingly empty space is actually an infinitely filled space, and that it must exist in some common denominator which will justify a true scientific relationship from one dimension to another, and relate all of this Infinite into a harmonious pattern of junctions and interpolations. Therefore let us begin our symposium upon a very simple equation which is contained in a familiar type of physical manifestation, by simply throwing a stone into the center of the pond; thus we can see the waves of energy stemming away from this point of impact where the stone entered the water and out into the surrounding area. By looking at some chips we have cast upon the surface of the water, we shall find that the water itself has not moved in any particular relationship to the center or the point of impact, except that it has moved up and down in a wave-like motion or in an oscillating manner. The chips always remain in the same place wherein they were first cast. We have thus begun to analyze that here again we have transferred energy from one particular point of perspective into another.

We can therefore begin with Infinity, in saying we
have an originating or an EMF source of force, or
motion, or intelligence, whichever it is that you wish
to superimpose into your consciousness, and that
stemming outwardly into an infinite number of types
of transferences are different kinds of manifestations
of energy wave forms. These types of energy forms, in
themselves, all portray individually, a certain junction
of relationship with the Infinite as it could be termed
intelligent, either positively or negatively. However,
unlike the waves which stemmed from the center of the
pond, energy does not travel from the central, or infinite source of supply, into the other dimensions in
these wave-like formations; instead, we will find energy is constantly regenerating itself into various types
of patterns which are cyclic in motion, or possess a
certain cyclic form. Each cycle in itself presents upon
its surface an undulating wave-like motion which is
composed of negative and positive wave formations
which are all portraying a certain kind of intelligence;
and in themselves, are linked and interlinked—just
as the wheels within a watch or the wheels within
a chain so we find these infinitely numbered cyclic
patterns stemming out into the various dimensions
about this originating source.

We shall not attempt, at the moment, to interject an
understanding of this originating EMF, for that, too,
presupposes in itself a certain junction of harmonic
patterns of transference into an even farther form of
Infinity; and with such an abstraction or understanding of such an Infinity, the Infinite would of course be
physically impossible with the presently existing terminating sources of consciousness as they are posed
upon the conscious mind. Thus, we see from this central or emanating source a great interplay or interchange of an infinite number of cycles of motion, each
in themselves linking arm-in-arm with their neighbors

and all relating in themselves an infinite number of patterns of various transferences of consciousness. These, in turn, regenerate into such harmonic structures as are compatible within themselves and other further extensions of such presupposed and concurrently existing forms of consciousness, or as were originally contained within the basic cycle or patterns of transference.

Herein enters the principle: in the regeneration of these various harmonic structures which is one of the creative principles impounded in Infinite Consciousness, there is bound to be within these various cyclic patterns of motion, certain junctions or combinations of junctions which are called parallaxes. At that particular point of terminus—as they are joined together in a certain combination of compatible unions of frequency relationship—there will be a certain hard core nucleus thus formed; comparatively hard, we shall say, because in common terms of reference, there are a large number of forms of consciousness being expressed in common union and at a common given point. In this hard core nucleus of consciousness, there sometimes originates certain vortical patterns which can be likened to the whirlwinds seen upon the desert. Here again is a certain pattern of regeneration as it stems down into a number of sub-infinities and, in the end, a certain terminus or terminal point wherein the vortex will focus itself into another form of the hard core nucleus, which can sometimes be entirely unrelated to the originating forms of consciousness as they were instigated by the higher forms of cyclic motion.

This can be compared in some respects to two known physical laws, which are called adhesion and repulsion. If we find two kinds of liquids perfectly merging as in the case of water and alcohol, we will find that here the molecules are adhesively related to each other and can blend quickly. Here, too, the case with atoms is quite synonymous and some atoms can merge very quickly with other kinds of atoms and form certain types of molecules. Conversely the same principle is applied in repulsion; that is, a small quantity of oil placed upon a surface of water will easily demonstrate that oil and water do not mix. This is simply because of the fact that in the electromagnetic fields of the atoms themselves are formed either compatible or noncompatible unions of energy transference and thus become either adhesive or repulsive.

The same principle takes place in the formation of vortexes in the regeneration of cyclic patterns of energy or motional transference in the higher dimensions. We now find that the terminating end of a vortex has, so far as the Infinite is posed above it in different dimensions, adapted within itself a certain cohesive form of relationship with its originating source of supply. Thus it cannot revert back into some original form of cyclic motion, but is further expelled, so to speak, from the parent supply in a common trajectory and again relates itself into some dynamic movement through what we presuppose to be space and time. It must be remembered here by the reader that the movement of space or time, as it relates to the Infinite, does not mean there is such a thing as space or time in the Infinite. It means that we, as individuals in our consciousness and in sustaining life upon the earth, have only assumed a certain movement of consciousness with Infinity, and as we are moving along this predetermined line of consciousness as it is posed in its cyclic motion, we are moving through Infinity at the rate of 186,210 miles per second which is the supposed rate of speed of light. Therefore, it is we who are moving in our consciousness and not the Infinite which is moving about us; and we are only terminating in the common denominator of space and time, a certain conjunctive relationship of consciousness with the Infinite.

When these particles of vortical energy thus become cohesive in their common terminating point, as they are thus expelled from the Infinite Cosmogony which so created them, they assume this same trajectory in regard to their former position in what we might call the terminating speed of light and thus are hurled into what the scientist calls free space. It means, so far as this tiny nucleus of energy is concerned, it is only trying, in its own way, to relive itself into Infinity, to again form within its own consciousness with a number of regenerative patterns and cyclic motions of transference, a common union or junction with its originating source.

This originating source can be said, so far as the common energy particle or cosmic ray is concerned, to exist anywhere in the Infinite because in the Infinite it can be presupposed that the originating sources of these energy forms can be terminating in vortexes simultaneously in an infinite number of points of terminus and in an infinite number of times per second. Thus, we have this great and abundant supply of tiny energy particles known as mesons, protons, or positrons and various other objective forms of energy coming into the earth's atmosphere, which are called cosmic rays or particles by the scientist.

This same principle in turn relates itself in a common form with the regeneration of every known so-called solid particle which science is able to equate upon a common atomic scale of interpolation. All common atoms, as they are thus posed by the scientist in this day, can be considered in their own way only as terminating points of certain vortical patterns regenerated from cyclic forms of motion from the Infinite Cosmos.

The foregoing is quite true with the formation of aggregates as they concern the earth, or in such larger junctions of aggregates as they concern a sun, either our own sun or one of the other suns in our galaxy or in our universe; in fact, the cyclic or vortical pattern of our universe is quite well known to modern-day astronomers. It, in itself, portrays very vividly the common pattern of cyclic motion which regenerated it from that great Infinite Cosmos and an infinite number of dimensions, and which the scientist cannot as yet see or determine in his present-day hypothesis either from the slide rule, calculus, or various other types of technical impedimenta.

Several years ago, a well-known scientist (Robert Oppenheimer), who is called the "Father" of the atom bomb, made a statement in a nationally known magazine that we had at that time reached the point of diminishing returns in our mathematical science. He further stated that any new advancement in technocracy of the various sciences would have to be made in directions which were yet unknown to the present-day scientist. Today has seen a partial justification of his prophecy; while man is struggling to hurl rockets into space or into orbit around the earth, he is going through the first stages of an entirely new and inceptive process of Infinite Cosmogony; and in the next few years, the scientist will realize the abysmal ignorance of trying to equate the whole Infinite in terms of third dimensional equation and mathematical formulae; therefore, he will become, through necessity, increasingly cognizant of this Infinite Cosmogony about him.

No attempt at this time, either in this chapter or in such succeeding texts, shall be made to enter into a full technical discussion as to equations, mathematical formulae, etc., for the simple reason that this work is intended to first spring the lock upon the dungeons

141

of the various material obsessions as they are contained in our present-day terrestrial dispensations, whether they were religious in nature or were so diametrically opposed to dogmas in our existing scientific concepts; that this work necessarily had to appeal not only to the scientists but to those who possess a much more prosaic form of interpretation of life about them.

The seeker who is trying to evaluate a more spiritual relationship to this Infinite Cosmogony about him has somehow, through evolution, sensed or he has been able to bring some nebulous form of consciousness into his present-day life dispensations. In the succeeding years, our technocracy will gradually develop into various formulas, pattern analysis, etc., which will more factually relate, in an integrated pattern, the concepts which are posed in this work. But first it is necessary for anyone so interested, not only in his own personal destiny into the future but also in the destiny of his fellow man, that he should be made aware of the existing principles of creation as they are more directly concerned with that infinite future into which he will progress through the succeeding evolutions and lives he will live in that future.

CHAPTER 20

In summing up the various concepts contained in the previous texts, it is hoped by now that the student has arrived at some rather important conclusions in his introspection of the Infinite, but it is always well that we should again enter into and review these most important factors of our relationship with the Infinite.

In the beginning it was posed that individually, man reflected in his earth life a certain negative polarity of transference of consciousness in respect to the Infinite, and herein enters at least one very important and dynamic concept which everyone should remember in the future. This is: nothing is static in the Eye and Mind of the Infinite; that all consciousness is constantly in motion and so far as the terrestrial or earth dimension is concerned—in terms and references to our modern science—can be considered energy wave forms which have a positive and a negative polarity as an oscillating motion. This was further equalized in our common objectivism, that by throwing a stone into a pond we could see energy being transferred in an undulating or an up and down motion from one point to another.

In common terms of reference, therefore, it is most important to remember that in all forms of motion, whether they are concerned with the more immediate terrestrial or third dimension, or into the more infinite abstractions, there is always involved the concept of polarity. This means that always within each form of consciousness, as it is expressed in such a wave

143

form or a motion, and whether or not it is contained in a point to point terminus, a third dimensional equivalent, or to more infinite abstractions as are contained in cyclic motions of transference within the cycle itself, there is always the resolution of the positive to negative and negative to positive equivalents of transference which always presents to the face of Infinity its own particular equivalent of consciousness as it was so regenerated from the vastness and the infinite beginnings of the most Infinite.

Throughout this vast interchange and this great sea of infinitely filled "void" which has been called space, we have seen this interplay of consciousness as it was contained in polarity patterns. These polarity patterns—whether they were related to forms of expressions as great cycles in which certain junctions are terminating points of consciousness as polarity transferences, or that they regenerated other commonly related vortical patterns within themselves—in turn, focused into a common terminating point called a sun, a galaxy or even a universe. Even the universe itself, in its general and known pinwheel-like fashion, was a silent voice telling the scientist how this great vortex—stemming from an infinite number of dimensions above it—was, in turn, only a very small and infinitely minded particle of consciousness which again linked and relinked, through a large number of infinitely vast cycles, into another form of consciousness which was so expanded in nature that it would indeed not only stagger your consciousness but would remain absolutely undetermined, so far as any particular points of introspection were concerned in your present attempt to evaluate this Infinite.

Conversely, the world of atoms and atomic forms as they are again subdivided into electrons and positrons are resolving themselves contra wise into configurations of polarity patterns; as the electron represents the negative quotient of the atom, while the positron, the hard core or nucleus. These are only determined in their position or relationship to the expression of consciousness with a similar vortex which supports them from another dimension. This vortex, in turn, then becomes a common form of expression which is again linked in that cyclic pattern of transference of consciousness into an increasing number of greater and more expanded forms of cyclic motion into this same Infinite Cosmogony. Thus we have again transferred polarity into two equally and infinitely expanded fields of consciousness into sub-infinity; and even the electron or the proton in turn would subdivide itself into Infinity in another direction, just as does vortical and cyclic motion transfer consciousness into Infinity into the expanded universe.

These principles of regeneration or reorientation of consciousness, as are posed in cyclic or vortical methods of transference of such forms of consciousness from various polarities, and thus contained within, are part of the regenerative process in the creation of each individual in whatever particular material or spiritual constituents which that individual is, at any time, expressing in his perspective to the Infinite. These same common principles, in all their abstractions and implications, involve an infinite number of creative forms of consciousness in which man will find himself in his travels into this Infinity. Thus in the future eons of time, he will find himself in other worlds and in other dimensions wherein introspection is carried into an increasingly larger number or into an entirely different realm and dimension of perspective than he is now immediately occupying.

To some degree, this journey into the future has been the common lot of those whom the religionists call Avatars or Masters, such as Jesus of Nazareth, or other such exponents of seemingly advanced forms of truth or consciousness in the histories of our world. These and other forms of consciousness, as they are transferred into other fields—such as science in its various branches—can also be truly interpreted as part of a more advanced form of consciousness related to any one, or a given number of individuals who have thus progressed beyond the boundaries of the immediate reactionary dimension, which is the common lot of all individuals who so occupy the earth at this particular time. Basically, and at nominal rates of transference, each individual, as he has been selected as representing the average individual concerned with an average materialistic life upon the earth, does pose within his conscious mind an advanced negative polarity which is biased entirely by the physical dimension into which he has passed, from succeeding life-times. He is also, to some degree in an intuitive fashion, negatively biased to the positive or the spiritual side of his dimension into the Infinite, and into which he will travel in future regenerations of consciousness wherein he will again occupy a physical body from time to time, in his attempt to evaluate and to reform the Infinite into some adjutants of physical consciousness.

Here again, another important principle has been activated and previously explained but does however, bear further mention. This is the common process of polarizing consciousness from one particular polarity to another as it is posed from the Superconsciousness of each individual; and its implications in vortical and cyclic patterns of consciousness, stemming from the Infinite into that exact configuration of the negative polarity as it is posed by an infinite number of lifetimes lived in physical or terrestrial dimensions of consciousness.

So, dear reader, it makes but little difference where

we transfer our particular point of perspective. To analyze and to equate the movements, transferences, and various interpolations of consciousness, as they are more directly concerned with an infinite perspective always means that we must involve the same relationship of such transferences into the common movements of cyclic and vortical patterns, as they relate each form of consciousness to its own particular position in regard to Infinity.

Thus, in the future, the scientist will be able to establish, not only from the physical dimension, a limited number of physical laws which were first posed by Newton in his laws of mechanical motion, but he will also be able to transfer his equivalents of analysis into perspectives and dimensions which involve a much greater number of dimensions of consciousness, and the transference of such forms of ideologies and expressions of life into common denominators which he will then, at that future time, call his existing physical science.

At that future date, he will then be able to equate in his own mind a more suitable manner in which to relate himself to the infinite vastness of space about him, and which seems only space at the present moment because he lacks the certain reactive senses to determine all values in this so-called space. Thus, in relating himself into more of these dimensional forms of transference as they are thus posed, in his future analysis he will see man living in various forms of relationships and in different dimensions involving other spectra of transferences.

At that future time—if he so deems it necessary to create such a suitable transitory vehicle as he calls a flying saucer—he will also be able to transform the basic vibrating rate of the atoms, as they are affected in gravitational fields of force or the electromagnetic fields of force about the earth, into other dimensions and thereby he will have automatically eliminated the now existing barriers of this seemingly impregnable vastness of space; and space in itself will at least have become partially nonexistent.

CHAPTER 21

In the future vistas of time, however, it can reasonably be supposed that the scientist will begin to
include the various concepts as they relate him to
Infinity and as they have been largely posed in the
various texts contained in this book. The progress of
science, even though it has been comparatively rapid
in the past fifty years, yet it is at the present moment
progressing at much less than a snail's pace, when it
can be evaluated upon some basis wherein a certain
degree or relative position to Infinity can be presupposed into our analogy.

Therefore, any seemingly strong statements which
have been placed in the text of this book are entirely
justifiable inasmuch as the author does not, in himself personally, take full moral responsibility for the
construction or for the evaluation of these texts and
has served only as a channel or a medium of transference into this outer world. He is not to be considered to be in any way, an irascible escapist who is a
misanthropist and hates all mankind; but he has
merely succeeded in elevating his consciousness to a
point where the world seems to be rather an abysmal
place of extreme ignorance and various other depri-
vations, which are always the result of retarded consciousness.

This too, has been the common lot of all of those
individuals who have gone somewhat beyond the
realms of the material dispensations of our physical
earth. To Jesus, this was also somewhat of a problem

and He often, in moments of feeling irritation, expressed himself to the materialists and called them thus,
"Thou hypocrites." For indeed mankind does become
a hypocrite, not only to the Infinite Creative Force
which has regenerated itself into all finite forms of
consciousness but he has also become—in his hypocrisy—his own worst enemy. He has retarded his advancement and his development; he has inflicted his
present terminating point of physical life with all
manners and forms of various intolerances, warlike
attitudes and other particular types of materialistic
derelictions which are actually more bestial in nature
than those exhibited by the prowling beasts of the
jungle.

In this way the pure science of our day, while it
may try to cover itself with a halo of glory by saying
that knowledge of atomic research is necessary, yet
primarily, atomic research was instigated purely
upon the basis that the armies of this nation had to
have a better weapon to kill their fellow men than
their fellow men possessed to kill them. Just how far
this reactionary condition will exist into the future,
will determine whether man shall live upon this planet,
or whether he shall blow it into "kingdom come".

There are also many other concepts which are indirectly proportions of relationships which have been
posed in the different texts and concepts contained
herein. The seemingly so-called molten core of iron
and nickel which the earth is supposed to have, is
another one of those fallacious renditions of our
physical sciences; and as far as the interior of the
earth is concerned, it does, toward the center, present
only to the outer or the exterior surface, an increasingly higher ratio of incidence of energy transference
from the vortex from which it stems. That which has
been seen and termed the hard crust of the earth is
only the exterior shell of a number of atomic energy

forms or constituents which have remained statically balanced, so to speak, revolving within their own orbits for the common expression of dynamic energy.

Conversely, then, the scientist will be able to find in the future—if he ever succeeds in getting down into the immediate exact center of his own earth—that it is quite likely to be just as much of a so-called vacuum as is the space about him. Unless he has certain determinants of various senses or developed factors or other particular scientific impedimenta which can determine these things for him, the energy forms which are contained in the interior heart of the earth—or in the exact center—will, at the present time, be beyond the realm of his present understanding, and he shall not be able to see into the interior, or the exact center of the earth, any more than he shall be able to see space about him.

Should this same scientist be able to levitate himself from the gravitational field of the earth into the space about him, in coming into a more direct contact with the sun and occupying a position about half way between these two stellar orbs, he will see that the earth, too, in certain ratios of transference, presents about it a certain field of force—a corona—and that he will find it extremely difficult and perhaps impossible to see the earth itself because of this highly supercharged static field of energy forms which surround the earth.

This is quite true in a somewhat different relationship with other planets in this solar system and particularly so of Venus. The chromosphere of the sun is merely a supercharged field of force which surrounds a much more dense and heavier planet within the confines of this external field of force; and on certain occasions, the gyrating motions of this energy field subdivide themselves and form small vortical patterns or holes which the scientist calls "sun spots", through which he can actually look and see the blackness within.

This should have definitely proven to the scientist a long time ago, as he studied the sun, that it was not hot; but that this force field, in common terms of relationship (as has been previously discussed), and through cyclic forms of transference into existing electromagnetic fields around the earth, was transforming into compatible frequency spectra—known as heat and light—its various energy constituents. The sun itself only represents, to a large degree, a catalizing EMF or stimulating force wherein these various forces, through cosmic hysteresis, were thus able to manifest themselves into various energy forms which are common to our science.

When man does possess a space vehicle, he will be able to travel, not only from here to the sun, but when he gets close to the sun, he will find it is not hot as he commonly presupposed it to be; he will be able just as other particular flying saucers from different parts of the galaxy or universe, to easily penetrate through this exterior chromosphere and land upon the interior surface of the planet itself, for the sun is truly a planet, in all respects. Just as the earth is a planet to the sun, the sun, in turn, becomes a planet to a larger portion of the galaxy, part of which is seen in the dimension of sight known as the Milky Way.

(Note: The text for this book was given in 1959)

CHAPTER 22

One other important concept which the student must always remember is that in his evolutionary flight through this so-called time and space in the reliving of a large number of lifetimes which, as they were in each succeeding life, pre-evaluated upon a common basic understanding of material values from one or a number, or all of the preceding lifetimes, he has thus largely developed various reactive mechanisms within his consciousness. He has thus, through these succeeding generations, placed himself directly in the line of transference of energy as a reactive element from one particular form of transference to another. In other words, through consciousness and its associations, he has thus adopted the human form, and this in turn relates him to such transferences of energy as heat; thus he can be burned.

Another reactive element also resides in atomic constituents which man finds about him. He can dig the iron ore from the earth, and after suitable smelting, form it into a sword which will again become a reactive element through his body. The same sword can, with other swords, again form a suitable instrument which can turn over the earth and therein grow crops to sustain his life upon this planet. The disposition here, and in the transferences as they are concerned in dispensations of consciousness to the average individual, then becomes its own prerogative. In this way man is largely different from any other particular form of species of plant or mammalia, as it is concerned upon our terrestrial planet. All other forms of plant and mammalia, to a large degree, form a more directly and commonly related pattern of transference in everyday life which is also presupposed and predisposed by previous incarnations. Only in man, however, do we find such wide deviations as are given in common terms of reference which are referred to as reason.

Reason, in itself, means that any particular individual has formed within the realm of his consciousness, a large number of conjunctions of energy transferences from any one or a number of more immediate terrestrial and spiritual dimensions about him; and in these junctions, transfers what he calls consciousness into such reactive elements of life about him. His spiritual life will, by this common evaluation and in this future symposium, then begin to embody by necessity in his future evolutions, certain forms of consciousness which can further reinstate him into other horizons of perspective as they are concerned with more spiritual forms of life and which do not include embodiment into a physical form of flesh. The problem of death will have, by that time, been completely alleviated, and will no longer be a form of consciousness which is feared by the material man. At that far distant future time, he will thus, in the common denominators of intelligence which are transferred into his consciousness in his daily life, relate himself to a more infinite perspective of consciousness as it concerns the Infinite which stems from that infinite Infinite.

This is cosmic continuum, and in every sense of the word it shall become the common property of each individual as he is thus revolving in some terrestrial dimension in the future, providing of course, he so wishes it to become a part of him and he is suitably inspired or preconditioned by conscious or subconscious memory transferences of spiritual lives which he has lived in the lives between lives. This will, in the future, form the necessary libido or drive, the joie de vivre, or the impetus to sustain his life into these infinite perspectives and horizons of consciousness which he will occupy in that future Infinity.

For the present however, let us begin to constructively evaluate life about us as to succeeding regenerations of consciousness into various cyclic forms as they are regenerated from the Infinite Consciousness. When this has become an integrated part of daily life, the fear of death and subsequent different inflictions of the terrestrial world will begin to disappear about us; problems relating to life in the physical consciousness will disappear, and in future regenerations and evolutions, you will find that the physical body, too, will have disappeared and that life then will be lived entirely in spiritual dimensions which are, at the present time, beyond your immediate dimension of consciousness. So, for the future, may you journey into this Infinity in full realization and in full consciousness of the regenerative principles of life which are constantly being manifest into your daily life.

CHAPTER 23

The presentation of the various concepts contained in the previous texts will present to the layman and the scientist alike, some rather obviously startling departures from the commonly accepted idioms of scientific knowledge which have been collectively propounded during the past hundred years or so, or since the beginning of our present-day physical science. It must be remembered however, that these concepts are not idle theorems or conjectures, but are indeed quite factual and can be proven by numerous existing mysteries, as well as the more commonly accepted forms of physical sciences as they now exist. It is our avowed purpose and intention to prove from such mysteries and unexplained paradoxes as now presently exist in our physical science and in the beginnings of this so-called new "space age", that these concepts are indeed correct.

For instance, it has been posed that the interior of the earth will present to itself, not the commonly accepted form of molten iron, as is supposed to exist in our modern understanding in the scientific world, but will actually—so far as present instrumentation is concerned—cease to be, or shall become nonexistent in that future day when the scientist succeeds in penetrating the thin crust of the earth. Yet, indeed, it must not be surmised that the interior of the earth is a vacuum, no more so than the infinitely filled solid space which surrounds the terrestrial planet earth, and which has been accepted by the scientist as space simply because he lacks the relative means to relay any particular dispensations of reactance or resistance into the horizon of his five senses.

When the scientist does penetrate the surface of the earth, should he have, at that time, the correct instrumentation to differentiate the various types of energy spectra which exist in or beneath the crust of the earth, he will indeed find that energy forms do surpass and go beyond the limits of his present-day understanding of atomic constituents in the scale of the some 100 atoms, of which he now presupposes his science to be compounded. In this way, we shall prove that the interior of the earth is not molten, but composed of regular layers or dimensions of energy, each one in an increasingly dense layer to the immediate layer above it. That, too is part of the vortical pattern as a hard core nucleus of a great vortex.

At this point, we shall bring into consciousness a very important and dominant factor of relationship which must be remembered by both the reader and the scientist in this analogy, as it concerns not only the interior of the earth, but the so-called space which surrounds the earth. Therefore, may we interject two very important findings which the scientist has made in the past few years, and which have to some extent, torn down or completely changed some previously existing scientific concepts; or these facts have presented, at the moment, some unexplained mysteries.

In shooting experimental rockets into orbit, the last stage or nose-cone is known as a satellite. Contained within these revolving spheres is certain radio apparatus which has been installed to transmit definite information back to the earth. In this respect, the scientist has found that to his knowledge no suitable mechanism exists which is capable of measuring temperatures as were previously supposed to have been known in this (so-called) space. In other words, thermometers or any other temperature measuring device remain completely inert when suitable distance is attained from the surface of the earth wherein there is a cessation of a certain interplay of cosmic energy transferences from other dimensions.

This brings a very important fact to bear, that all known scientific apparatus, as it so exists, has been developed from a comparatively limited band of energy interpolations which can be considered to present (in our evaluation), a means or, in other words, a certain definite point from which he can equate or equalize such existing physical phenomena as is apparent in our daily life and which is reactive to some degree, to the five existing physical senses. However, this does not presuppose—as we have postulated in other texts in this book—that there are not an infinite number of various interpolations of energy and transduction which exist in an infinite number of dimensions and to which the five senses are in no way sensitive.

Thus the scientist is finding that his present-day apparatus, as it is so concerned with the means of the five physical senses, presents a very limited and narrow perspective or horizon of introspection. He has thus become confounded by the fact that his temperature measuring devices are now not reactive outside the confines of the atmospheric envelope of the earth and its statically surcharged field of force. This force field is a byproduct of the various generic forces as they move in the magnetic lines of force surrounding the earth, and link it (cosmically speaking), to the infinite universe.

It might also be noted at this time, that should the scientist succeed in levitating a man above the surface of the earth and out into space at a sufficient distance, he would (as it has been suggested in a previous text), find that the picture of the earth would be quite

158

similar to that of the planet Venus. He would not be able to see the exact surface of the earth, simply because of the various intervening layers and fields of force of surcharged or ionically charged particles of matter which are more correctly called electrons.

Therefore in establishing within the dimensions of our consciousness, science in its present existing state, is only interpolating into consciousness, as the perimeter of the five conscious or physical senses, the known horizon of the physical science. By this token then, should the scientist penetrate the crust of the earth, he would most certainly lack the correct instrumentation to determine any reactive constituents, as they might manifest themselves in any existing instrumentation which he might now possess.

Here again enters another supporting concept which presently presents a great paradox to the scientist, for he has found in his laboratory, ways and means to subject various atomic forms—such as copper—to the temperature of absolute zero, which is approximately, 472 degrees below zero. In this lowered state of temperature (and we use the word "temperature" rather loosely), the scientist has found that the copper has now a perfect conductivity and presents no reactance or resistance to the electric force which may be passing through it at that particular moment. This is in direct contradiction to the Ohms law, which means that again when the scientist, Ohm, postulated his theory of resistance, he did so from the same commonly discussed base or means, as is relevant to the transposition of energy forms in the dimension of our five physical senses.

Herein enters a very important part of this concept. It must be firmly envisioned by the reader that atomic forms, as they present themselves on the surface of man's consciousness and to such various existing forms in his terrestrial dimension (or physical world), are all, in themselves, atoms—merely very minute transducers—that is, they are very busily engaged like small firemen in shoveling coal onto the fire, so to speak. The earth, as it presents itself to the physical man, maintains some sort of a mean temperature. This, too, is partially a byproduct from the transduction of energy from the fourth or fifth dimensional planes next to the earth, into the various atomic constituents of which it is so comprised.

The exact manner of transference of energy from the sun is not complete insofar as the earth is concerned; that is, it obtains energy in many different ways and forms as a direct result of transduction from many other dimensions, manners, and means. The reader may visualize that the planet earth, as it has been suggested, represents only the nucleus of a gyrating field of force which, in itself, has precipitated certain negative energy wave forms in an increasingly hard or dense core toward the center. These wave forms will, in turn, in this compressed relationship to the Infinite, form the various atomic constituents as one of the byproducts of this regenerative process. In the outward expansion into the third dimension, which presents a negative surface to this hard core of the vortical spectrum above it, is another of these regenerative byproducts, as seen in the expression of certain lines of force which are called magnetic lines of force. These in themselves, can be considered as primary channels of energy transference from one given dimension to another. They are, to some extent, governing reagents of the transductance of various types of energy from one dimension to another.

The earth, just as any other heavenly body including the sun, can therefore be envisioned within the mind as a huge atom. While the tiny core or the nucleus of the atom is at least partly responsible for maintaining a certain means within the five physical

160

senses, in the transduction of energy into the physical world, each atom can thus be considered a transducer. It is, as has been suggested, taking a certain quanta of energy from another dimension and, in the oscillating process, regeneratively speaking, in the manner and fashion of the vortex which comprises the earth itself, becomes an exact subparticle or facsimile of this same vortical pattern as the earth. Therefore, the atom can be considered in its function to be sending energy, or shooting energy off into the same lines of magnetic transference, as does the earth itself—or the vortex which forms the earth—in the function of the normal transductance of energy into the various physical relationships which comprise the atomic constituents of the earth itself. Therefore, the atom retains the correct mean temperature, as do all similar atoms, whether they are compounded in large or small quantities of the so-called neutronic, protonic elements, or surcharges, as they have been pictured by the atomic scientists.

It is quite obvious that a loaded vehicle cannot transport an additional load. If we load a one-ton truck with one ton of metal, it would then be very laborious to carry any additional load which was imposed upon it. The atom is in the same position, relatively speaking, as it is when contained in a long rod which can be called a copper wire. Each tiny atom composing a molecule or a crystal of copper is busily engaged at full capacity in transforming energy from one dimension to another to keep it as a copper atom within this certain mean temperature, or terrestrial dimension, into which it has so manifested itself. Any additional load in the form of energy, traveling at the rate of 186,000 miles per second, presents an additional load which it can, to some extent, laboriously conduct within the circumference of the magnetic lines of force of which it is comprised.

This represents the resistance, postulated by Ohm in his law of "Ohm's resistance". When the same atom which is contained in the copper wire is subjected to intense refrigeration or, to state more factually, an isolation process wherein the atom has been at least temporarily suspended or isolated from its interdimensional activity, it then becomes, to any outside force of traveling energy as it is reflected to it, a perfect conductor; simply because it is, in its own intelligence (its own I.Q.), ready, willing and able to assume the load which has been temporarily suspended from its activity due to the isolation by the so-called refrigeration.

In other words, so far as this individual atom is concerned, refrigeration and its subjugation to the absolute mean, so far as the scientist is concerned with 472 degrees below zero, it is, in effect, thrown a million miles away from the surface of the earth, out into another dimension in which it is not functionally active and does not perform its major task or its particular intelligence, in relating energy from one dimension into another.

The presentation of these facts and the seeming mysteries of present-day science should now clear up certain definite and pertinent points in the readers' introspection. As it was previously postulated, there is no such thing as space; it is infinitely filled and infinitely solid, so far as energy is concerned. This energy, in itself, assumes a vast magnitude and an infinite number of different forms and dispensations, as well as interchanges. This cannot be considered, in any way, to be a chaotic maelstrom but rather, a very highly organized interplay of energy forms which are transposing and transducing energy from one dimension into another by the simple and presently recognized laws of harmonic structures and the regenerative processes which are concerned when a large energy source is involved by the Infinite Mind in these various interpolations.

The world in itself, as well as the planetary system, the galaxy and the universe in which the earth is so situated, presents to even the most casual observer, a very obvious fact: there is much more to science at the present time than has been presupposed in any scientific dispensations. The vague and nebulous theories as they are posed by science—that any planet or sun represents in its formation, a long-term period of the collection of many tiny dust particles from space —is quite infantile and completely refutes any of the existing knowledge or laws of electronic force or motion. The various suns, stars, solar systems and galaxies only represent certain terminating points in the dispensations of energy wave forms and energy manifestations in the interdimensional expansion and contraction process. These planetary systems, as well as the universes themselves, represent only certain conjunctions or parallaxes, which can be considered as certain terminating points for a large number of energy wave forms from other dimensions which have reached a common junction and which are terminating and re-expressing themselves in the common laws of multiple harmonics into a secondary or lower dimension of transference.

The theory then, as postulated by modern science, that energy, heat or light comes from the sun, is in this respect not only completely inaccurate but bespeaks of the abysmal ignorance from which science is presently trying to levitate itself. When the future scientist begins to understand that the physical dimension (whether it is the earth, the solar system, or the universe about him), represents only an infinitesimally small point of energy transference from the Infinite into his present perspective or means of the five senses, he shall then begin to understand the

163

universal cosmogony, as it is more thoroughly understood by mankind in other planetary systems and in other dimensions.

The mention of cosmic dust and the fallaciousness that dust could exist in an infinitely filled space would, in itself, be a contradiction and a refutation of all known scientific principles of electronic force in motion. This brings us more directly to another of the most thoroughly misunderstood of the present-day scientific concepts and that is the weather.

It is generally believed and postulated by scientists who are supposed to know about such things, that rain or such precipitation is caused by the accumulation of moisture molecules upon some floating dust particles in the atmosphere immediately surrounding the cloud layer. This, again, is one of the infantile suppositions which also smacks of the utter and abysmal ignorance of which the scientist is guilty, in his failure to understand some very obvious processes of energy transferences which are a part of his daily life.

Precipitation from any layer of surcharged atmosphere, as it presents a large incidence of moisture particles, is possible only under certain conditions which can be classed in the general classification as ionization. In common laws, in the interpolation of energy from one dimension to another, various layers of gas above the surface of the earth represent in their atomic constituents, transductive elements.

The variance of these transductive elements, while small, yet are, in themselves, quite subjective to extra-terrestrial forces with which they are working, such as various differences in magnetic stresses which are fluctuating from the sun itself. Under such conditions, therefore, magnetic lines of force can be considered as a force, which when coming in contact with suspended layers of atomic particles represent certain conductivity in different spectra and which the scientist has called heat or light. Thus they can become charged negatively or positively with a temporary charge of magnetic energy and become ionized. Under such conditions, these particles attract other particles to them, representing negative polarities. When a sufficiency of these ionized particles are thus collected together, they also begin the process of collecting other suspended particles which are represented by denser particles as moisture, then precipitation begins.

This will also explain what the weatherman calls the various types of inversions, which mean high or low pressure areas. They simply represent (to a large degree), certain particular points wherein magnetic lines of force have an energy force, either compressed or released pressure, from the various points of these existing layers of gaseous atmosphere, thus generating the so-called high and low pressure areas. This means that only at these particular points, conductivity is either lessened or is increased, thus regenerating as a direct product, the ionization and the precipitation, or conversely in the other or more negative form, the arid or dry spells wherein there is no precipitation.

At this point, it should be quite obvious to the layman and scientist alike, that in the presentation of these different concepts, there is indeed much more to life than is commonly supposed from our present existing science, which has been basically determined from the various reactionary values as to their effect upon the five physical senses. It should also be quite obvious, especially to the scientist, that our present-day science is comparatively new, that is to say, perhaps less than one hundred years old; and so far as any other or previously existing sciences as they were postulated in such previous civilizations or epochs of time, were in themselves, almost completely sterile of the real and important values of life. In this sense, it can therefore be considered that our present-day science is the beginning of a new age.

In his future evolutions and the thousands of years to come, in the configurations of these various evolutions, man will pose either individually or collectively to the races of mankind as they come and go upon the surface of the earth; he will become increasingly aware of the great preponderance and interdimensional relationships which are in the world about him and which, in themselves, are in no way immediately related in a reactive sense to his five existing physical senses. This, then, can be considered to be a return to an age or a civilization which has long ago passed from the surface of the earth wherein man, in a similar cycle of transposition in his position to the Infinite, was so posed in his physical and spiritual sciences that he had begun to understand much more realistically his position to this Infinite than the scientist of today so relates himself.

It is also quite reasonable to suppose that in the vast galaxies and universes which populate this seeming "void" about us in our tiny nucleus of energy— which we call the earth—man can also be seen to be living in countless other dimensions far beyond his own "imagination", which is primarily concerned only as reactive elements within the subconscious mind, formed of terrestrial experiences from out of the past.

Therefore, any sane or intelligent man cannot at any time in his suppositions, ever lay down lines of demarcation for either physical science or any other particular relationships of mankind in the transposition of life about him. If he does so, he is only advertising his profound ignorance to his fellow mankind. There are no lines of demarcation as far as the Infinite is concerned, but relate only to successive relationships wherein certain predetermined spectra of energy transferences so reside which can be called dimensions. Such dimensions are so divided as to obtain the proper reciprocative action in their cosmic interplay, as generative and regenerative substances of energy or entities of intelligence.

Intelligence in itself, whether portraying any singular act of transposition in such interplay of energy, can thus be considered intelligent; and any accumulation of such intelligent wave forms can be considered, not only as an entity but also as a configuration. When such configurations become more vast and complex in their nature as to encompass various other dimensions or spectra of interpolations, then these can be considered to be individuals.

No man exists by the five physical senses alone. The tiny atoms of which man's body is composed, in the various processes of life about him whether they are of the more tangible, called the reactive elements of thinking, or of the more subjective reactionary forms of motion (such as walking, eating, etc.), can also be considered to be transduced forms of intelligent relationship, which he has either manifested from one or a number of previous experiences and the accumulation thereof, or they can be considered separate entities of expression in which he has attuned himself into the infinite void about him.

At this point too, it can be seen how fallacious is the commonly accepted form of science which relates man to a terrestrial dimension in which he is, as a flesh and blood being, so subjected to the entirety of life as it exists within the confines or means of his five physical senses. These five physical senses could not exist if it were not for such proper interdimensional frequency relationships which stem from such centers as the psychic body, and which have been previously constructed by this same individual in various lifetimes. Also, these psychic centers, in themselves, present attunements into various interdimensional configurations of entities or intelligent forms, equations and values of life which make his progression into the future possible by constantly presenting to the individual in his daily life, a never-ending succession of new experiences. While these things, in themselves, are all autosuggestive of past life experiences, yet they always pose in their transposition, an increasingly large number of ramifications which involve higher transpositions of energy forms of life in the higher dimensions.

The scientist who has developed the various testing devices for measuring the difference in the reactive or resistive values in his existing science, has in a sense already added to the confusion which exists in his own mind and which has come to him from the development of past lifetime experiences. This instrumentation and this science will not increase but will decrease his knowledge of the Infinite, for with the continued usage of such science, he will only more firmly entrench himself deeper into the mire of his terrestrial dimension.

Therefore, dear reader, when we gaze into the darkness of the summer night and see the luminous orb of the moon or the countless stars as pinpoints of light as they are presented in the vast distance of interstellar space, let us see, not with the physical eye, but with the inner eye, into the actual configurations of energy forms as they exist in this seeming void about us. Let us see those great magnetic lines of force which stretch like luminous ribbons, crisscrossing each other across the night sky. Let us see that the earth, the moon or the sun presents not only a singular ball of suspended energy or mass in space but that it presents in itself, the interior surface of a vast interplay of cosmic force which stems from many dimensions above it. In these gyrating, pulsating oscillations of radiant energy in the interior of this vast interplay of cosmic energies, we see our little earth, our little moon, or our still quite small sun.

Let us see ourselves, not as creatures of happenstance of some unfathomable bestial passion, regenerated from out of the earthly dust and its constituents and traveling to an unknown and unmarked grave; but let us see ourselves as entities of intelligence, compounded by an infinite and innumerable number of various conjunctions of other intelligent entities, which are stemming from these same infinite numbers of dimensions about us. Let us see ourselves as energy forms, pulsating just as does the sun, the moon, the earth and all of the stars into our own particular set of infinite relationships. Let us see that we are continually remanifesting upon the conscious surface of our mind these innumerable and different dispensations of experiences which we call life and which represent in themselves, only a part of that over-all regenerative, resurgent pattern of intelligence called God, which represents the Infinite.

When we have thus attained this new perspective and we have widened our horizons to include the vastness and the infinite number of vistas of life as they are so compounded from the various and innumerable number of dimensions which are a part of this Infinite, then we shall have indeed become men. We shall have taken the part in the scale of evolution which was primarily designed—if it can be so conceived—as this plan for each and every individual, that he, in himself becomes an oscillating polarity to the infinite whole. He will, in his future evolutions, thus manifest an increasingly larger number of horizons or dimensions of interplay with this Infinite. Only then can he be considered a man. When he is thus a man, he can be considered a master for he has, in this new perspective and in the widening of his horizon, included the Infinite and arrived at that point where he has indeed become an oscillating polarity with the Infinite in all of the ramifications which would involve such an interchange of polarity patterns.

We should not resign ourselves to the common form of life which is subject to disease; to various reactions of social and political systems; to the vicissitudes of vice and corruption which propound these terrestrial civilizations. Instead, let us take our place in the Infinite as intelligent constituents which, in ourselves as separate entities, are compounded of various infractions of these interdimensional forms of consciousness. We will then have assumed our proper role to the Infinite; and yet even the Infinite is not all, for once we have attained what we might, at this particular point called Infinite Consciousness, we shall indeed again be confronted with an increasingly vast horizon or a prospect for attainment, for such is the way; there is no ending, no cessation. Indeed, this is the principle of life itself, the dynamic and never-ending interplay of consciousness into an infinite number of forms and an infinite number of relationships; and only in this way can the Infinite live, can It become a part of everything. In the various transpositions of life in our journey into this Infinite, we thus become a part of It and can thus be considered spiritual beings, the True Men, Created of Spirit.

ADDENDUM

Inasmuch as it has been about a year since dictating this book, it would be well to note at this time, various scientific discoveries which have happened since that time, the presentation of these present-day scientific findings together with some other existing facts pertinent to that dimension of scientific research known as geophysics, astrophysics and astronomy. These facts and figures will give you, the reader, a more comprehensive understanding of the word Infinite, as it has been repeated so many times in the previous pages. The greatest amount of emphasis must therefore be placed on understanding the Infinite.

Much of our present-day information and findings came out of the International Geophysical Year, a united international scientific effort, participated in by most nations of the world in an attempt to increase man's span of knowledge of the great macrocosm. The I.G.Y. was an 18-month period of time between the first of July 1957 and December 31, 1958, and all of the data compiled during that time has not as yet been completely evaluated.

Space probes in the form of satellites, balloons, rockets, etc., have also added considerably to this already existing fund of knowledge. It is interesting to note that it was found the mean circumference of the earth was within a few miles of the same figure as that given by the Greek physicist and astronomer Eratosthenes of Cyrene, more than 2,000 years ago.

Democritus, too, near that time, posed the theory that the earth revolved around the sun and that the nebulous light from the Milky Way was actually a composite of light infiltrations made up from billions of stars.

During the first thousand years A.D., the Arabs and other mid-Eastern nations were teaching their children a comparatively advanced astronomy. In contrast, all Europe, as a part of the Christian dominion, was living in complete abysmal ignorance of any kind of a comprehensive physiology and astronomy. As late as the 18th century, people were being burned to death at the stake or tortured at the rack and wheel for believing in and teaching physiological and astronomical concepts which were not a part of the liturgy of the Holy Roman Church.

In the Middle Ages, popes, cardinals, bishops, monks, nuns and priests, as well as school teachers, all taught that the earth was God's footstool; it was square and at each of the four corners, an angel was holding it up while the heavens revolved around it.

Copernicus was the first major luminary to preach against these asinine astronomical concepts. Others like Galileo followed in their work to illuminate the western world. It is also interesting to note that in the 16th century, a certain Catholic Archbishop, Usher of Armagh, definitely established the creation as having taken place in the year 4002 B.C. This ridiculous assumption was later verified by Bishop Lightfoot, another luminary of the church who not only agreed upon that year but also gave the exact day and minute.

How great indeed is the contrast between this narrow-minded Middle Ages bigotry and our present-day knowledge of our earth and universe. Perhaps it might be well at this moment to go into some facts and figures which are currently available and which are part of the curriculum taught in the various science classes in schools throughout the western nations.

Our tiny earth is one of nine major planets revolving around a central star or sun. This sun is one of the dwarf suns which shine in our own major galaxy or universe and which is a disc-shaped rotating sea of some 30 billion stars or suns looking somewhat like a pinwheel. Some idea of the size of this galaxy can be visualized when we realize that light, traveling at 186,210 miles per second, takes 100,000 light years to travel from one edge to the other, and at the center part or the hub, is 10,000 light years thick. It also takes light 315,000 light years to travel around the complete circumference. Moreover, this galaxy is expanding and some other galaxies photographed by astronomers are speeding away from us, out into space, at more than 200 million miles an hour.

It is also estimated that our own solar system is traveling toward the outer edge of our galaxy at about 600,000 miles per hour. Looking further out into space and using not only giant telescopes but also the more newly-developed radio-telescope, the astronomer has found more than 6,000 million other galaxies and he is just beginning to count them. Remember also that our nearest neighboring galaxy is more than one million, five hundred thousand light years away and if you could travel one million miles an hour, it would take you about 3,000 years to reach the nearest star which is four and one-half light years distant.

Of course these figures are meaningless to the third dimensional mind. One important fact, however, does remain uppermost, that in space it is now well-known that certain physical bodies like suns and galaxies are traveling at more than twice the speed of light and this fact has already vindicated one of the concepts postulated in this text: that the speed of light is only a divisional quantum of energy expressed from one dimension to another.

Returning to our more immediate environment, the earth, it has been found by scientists using rockets and satellites, that about six to ten thousand miles above the earth, there are at least two large radiation belts which encircle the earth like bands. It has also been found that 100 miles above the earth, the mean temperature at the north and south poles was higher than at the equator (100 miles above the earth).

Another discovery made by the I.G.Y., that the sky as seen above the atmosphere contains numerous sources of ultra-violet light, which appear as diffused nebulosities—proof that the cosmic ray flux is markedly increased in intensity at the time of sun spot maximum, indicating the existence of magnetic fields in interplanetary space, verification that auroral displays contain electrons and ions.

These facts again partially vindicate certain other concepts presented in the context of this book, that such energy as is considered heat and light which supposedly comes from the sun in a straight line transference, is entirely erroneous and that energy from the sun is converted into heat and light through magnetic hysteresis from various magnetic lines of force interconnecting the sun and earth as well as all other heavenly bodies and all such energy does not come as a direct line transference but is resolved into a cyclic motional transference.

Also, the sun, like all other suns and planets, are apexes of great vortexes of energy; giant centrifuges of interdimensional energy which fills this so-called space, resolve themselves not only into giant galaxies, but lesser vortexes become suns, and smaller vortexes within the vortex of the sun become hard-core nuclei called planets. This is the true construction of the infinite macrocosm.

Some day it is quite probable that the scientist will have a much more accurate picture of this Infinite than he now possesses and when that day arrives, "Cosmic Continuum" will be completely vindicated.

ADDENDUM NO.2

It is generally observed and conceded that during the past 60 years, man has achieved the greatest and most significant advances in various cultural sciences since the beginning of historical anthropology. This is particularly true in the realm of the classical sciences and, with this rapid development of these various sciences, mankind has been literally whisked from out of the complacent horse and buggy days of the "gay 90's" and plunged into a mad, roaring, screaming world of automation where he is now living a veritable robot-like existence.

In this era, we have witnessed many rapid and startling changes and with their coming, the old life passed away. With modern means of communication, any point on this globe is but hours or minutes away. Perhaps the greatest and most significant changes, however, have occurred within the framework of the pure classical sciences themselves, for within the various associated fields of physics, chemistry, aeronautics, astrophysics, astronomy, etc., have come many new and important concepts and with their coming, old laws and old concepts have also passed away.

After the close of World War II, great strides were made in the science of nuclear physics and with the development of various nuclear devices and weapons, activity in this field tapered off and was replaced by the new space age and its adjunctive developments in rockets, satellites, etc., all of which was tremendously activated in competition with the communist world.

As of today, this new space age has been brought about, not only through the competitive efforts in rocketry, but great emphasis and activity has been entered into collectively by many nations of the world in the field of pure astronomy and associated astrophysics; and perhaps no other field of science has witnessed so many rapid changes and developments which are going on in this ever-changing world.

Almost over night, and sometimes hour by hour, theories and values change as scientists probe with their telescopes and satellites into the great unknown voids everywhere about us; and as of this time, no real valid or comprehensive configurations exist as to what constitutes the great universe which stretches out into the dim unknown. This is a general opinion currently shared not only by astronomers, but by any sundry individuals who are keeping abreast of these rapidly changing developments.

A complete verification of our present-day invalid astronomical science was made in a public exposé over a national television network March 26, 1960, by a group of three eminent astronomers and one physicist, who were respectively, Dr. Fred Hoyle, (British astronomer), Drs. Allen Sandage and Jesse Greenstein and Dr. William Fowler (California physicist), in an hour-long program. These eminent savants climaxed the show in a mild conflict of opinions which involved, chiefly, the manner in which our universe was created and its age. These men did agree, however, on one pertinent issue, that by and large, all stars or suns which could be seen or photographed, were primarily of the same chemistry or atomic constituents.

We will neglect for the moment, the interjection of vast astronomical distances and enter more directly into the other issues—namely, the age and method of the creation and its countless billions of galaxies, star clusters, and stars.

At the present time, there seem to be two theories for this creation. One is called the "Big Bang" theory which goes something like this: at some long ago time —8 billion or more years ago—there existed a tremendously big ball of condensed energy; then, like some huge celestial firecracker, this thing exploded, scattering galaxies and stars all over the universe and where, theoretically, they have been spreading out ever since.

This theory is of course invalid on several counts. First, on such an explosion, such objects would be hurled away from the center in a straight line and it is known that our universe rotates just as do the various galaxies. Moreover, it is now known that our universe is filled with strong magnetic lines of force which are curved in a pin-wheel fashion, just as are those seen in various galaxies like our own. One more point; it is also known that the further away any particular galaxy is from us, the faster it is traveling away from us. Our own galaxy is proceeding on a curved line out into the unknown at about 600,000 miles per hour. Other galaxies further out are known to be traveling at two million miles per hour. In any explosion, any object traveling away from the center of the explosion constantly loses speed, not gains it.

The second, or "Steady State" theory of creation, while more valid is still incomplete. This theory postulates that from the center of the universe or some unknown point, new galaxies and new stars are constantly being created where, after a few billion years or so, they gradually die or fade away. And while they are so living their cycle, they somehow strangely become accelerated toward the outer unknown periphery of the universe. What gives these stars or galaxies this constantly accelerated speed is still unknown; and we may ask, where and what is the original source and origin of any energy which comes into our visible universe?

The presentation of this existing evidence which was discussed on this television program, shows that our present-day science of astronomy is still in complete and abysmal ignorance of the Creative Forces, not only in the field of astronomy and the macrocosm but in nuclear science or the microcosm.

Let us take for example the "Steady State" theory of the creation of the universe and, with a clear and lucid explanation, fill in the obvious lacking elements which would complete this theory into a rational fact. If the astronomer could picture a tremendously vast vortex of energy which existed in the more immediate 4th, 5th and 6th dimensions, where, in this great centrifuge, tremendous forces were at work through a certain positive and negative relationship as posed by various polarities of wave forms of energy compounding this vortex, certain movements take place which can be likened to the action of centrifugal and centripetal forces.

In other words, while positive energies travel toward the periphery, other more negative energies travel toward the center, becoming more compact or dense and more negative as they approach this center. Within the very center, energy is extremely compressed, so much so that a certain amount of transductance takes place into the third dimension. Vast curved magnetic lines of force stem out into the third dimension and, like the power lines from a powerhouse, conduct some of this compressed energy into our third dimensional universe; first in the form of simple electrons and protons which, in a commonly formed eddy current, assume the form of hydrogen atoms; great masses of these hydrogen atoms through certain pressures known as ionization are brought together into vast tenuous nebulosities called galaxies.

These cloud masses and hydrogen atoms are being constantly impelled away from the central core by a tremendous repulsive force, which is actually the flow of electromagnetic energy composing the great magnetic lines of force which all flow toward a common terminating polarity at the periphery of the universe. As these cloud masses are expelled away from the center, the ionization of positive and negative particles in the formation of hydrogen atoms begin to form nuclei; these collect and grow larger, eventually forming a star or sun. In this aggregate process of positive ionization, polarization also occurs in varying distances from the sun. These negative polarities form the planets. Not all suns form planets simply because in the rapid steady rate of expansion, great magnetic turbulence occurs which sometimes breaks up these various planetary polarities where they disintegrate into the semi-gaseous form, to again be used as new material.

This magnetic turbulence will also explain a nova, for here again ionization and polarization are vastly speeded up to a point where a burning out occurs. The star flares up and disappears. Magnetic turbulence will also explain pulsating stars, for here it can be seen that a certain cyclic motion is involved in the ionization and polarization process. Expansion from the central vortex, as has been previously explained, will also compensate for the differences in speeds of stars and galaxies from the center into the unknown, for as these heavenly objects proceed along the curved or bent magnetic lines of the universe, the universe is also rotating, following the same direction of rotation, but at a lesser rate of speed than the vortex which formed it.

Everyone knows that an object traveling on the rim of a wheel travels much faster to complete one revolution than does an object nearer the center of the wheel. Therefore, as the universe rotates, any galaxy constantly accelerates in speed as it progresses further out toward the periphery.

The galaxies themselves are primarily formed in vortexal fashion as the result of vast eddy currents which are interplaying among themselves in their magnetic fields. The galaxies, as spiral nebulae, can be pictured somewhat like a snowball rolling down hill. The galaxy is rotating between tremendous lines of force; the principles involved here are quite similar to those found in an alternating current motor.

As for the suns and stars themselves, the same process of synthesis is taking place to form the various known atomic constituents. The same gyrating centrifugal and centripetal forces always create and sustain any atom from the immediate fourth dimension.

Not all energy which stems from the central vortex becomes atomic material. In the process of this vast cosmic hysteresis, many of these units of energy which can be called electrons or protons, fly off into the free space of the third dimensional world. These tiny particles or electronic bullets, upon entering earth's atmosphere are known as cosmic rays; likewise the strong magnetic lines of force extending from the central vortex in conjunction with other such similar vortexes, create an infinitely vast and complex system of magnetic lines of force, all of which go to make up the controlling forces to hold various planets in their various orbits around their respective suns, as well as controlling the shape and ultimate destiny of various galaxies in this great universe.

One more point must be made: before his demise, Einstein presented to the world the theory of space-time continuum, wherein he mathematically proved that the speed of light, 186,210 miles per second, was nonexistent in space and that light could and did accelerate four or five times that speed. If Einstein was correct, what then becomes of all the known mathematical computations which astronomers have made regarding the distances found in our universe?

How can the modern astronomer correctly evaluate the temperature of some star by using the method of inversed proportions, figured on the basis of candlepower light which comes to the earth, sometimes millions of years after it started its journey? It is clearly indicated that at the present time the astronomer like the nuclear physicist, is hopelessly entangled in a web of intangibles and the further he proceeds along the false lines of his various assumptions, the more inextricably enmeshed he becomes. As far as the future is concerned, it will remain for the scientist of the future age to cut these Gordian knots and to present to himself and mankind a factual and realistic composite science based upon an understanding of creation which begins in the higher and presently unknown dimensions.

Inasmuch as the question may be raised as to what is the common terminating point of the cosmic universe, this means that in the expansion of this universe, a point begins to be reached where the magnetic lines of force again relink themselves with the positive corresponding polarities of the upper fourth dimensional vortex, something similar to positive and negative magnetic line linkage observed with a common horseshoe magnet. At the point where the lines of force begin to bend into the fourth dimension, all atomic constituents following these lines of force will begin to disintegrate back into their original energy constituents. (This bending will explain the known curvature of space.) This disintegration can be seen in such elements as radium and uranium, the older of the known elements which have already begun their disintegration and subsequent reabsorption back into the fourth dimensional Infinite.

Someday the astronomer may find a neighboring and similar universe and which does, in the same sense of polarity interactions, form the structural network of magnetic lines which makes energy conductance from higher dimensions into third dimensional forms possible; also such subsequent atomic constituents as elements which are the inductive facsimiles of this great cosmic evolution.

This, then, is the cyclic evolution of creation, a way in which the Infinite Creator, whom people call God, regenerates Himself and makes of Himself every visible and invisible form and substance known to mankind. When, in some distant future, mankind can universally see this great creation in action—religions, wars and associated dogmas and creeds, together with the lusts and bigotrys will largely disappear from the minds and hearts of men and in the place of these materialistic elements will be superimposed an abundant free-masonry of mankind which will make not only stellar space travel possible but will give all men who so understand, an access door into the higher Spiritual Realms of Light.

*   *   *   *   *

*Because of the vast and intricate complexities of the cosmic universe, the foregoing addendum was presented in a more easily understood form; a sort of thumbnail sketch. In future presentations planned by the author, a more thorough and complete dissertation will be entered into.

So far as the astronomical findings contained in Addendum No. 1 are concerned, these figures were drawn from currently existing astronomical suppositions and the author does not vouch for their accuracy. More accurate facts and figures will not be coming to the astronomer so long as he attempts to evaluate the vast Creative Cosmogony on the basis of known third dimensional reactive formulas.

Such computations are only relative and fall almost as fast as they are created. For instance, on the aforementioned television show, a pertinent issue involved was the age of the universe; a few years ago this age was thought to be 2 billion years, based on the theoretical evolution of the uranium atom. Today believers in the "Big Bang" theory state that it is at least 8 and possibly 13 billion years old; and one of the doctors on the aforementioned show is now bringing forth a new evaluation of 24 billion years, based on the assumed life cycle of a certain bright star.

To the future, then, we salute the new day which will bring forth a new and better science and understanding of the Creative Universe.